The Five-Year Century

MIHIR SHUKLA / NANCY HAUGE

The Five-Year Century

BOLD LEADERSHIP AND ACCELERATED OUTCOMES IN THE AGE OF AI

WILEY

For general information on our other products and services or for technical support, please contact our Customer Care Department within the United States at (800) 762-2974, outside the United States at (317) 572-3993 or fax (317) 572-4002.

Wiley also publishes its books in a variety of electronic formats. Some content that appears in print may not be available in electronic formats. For more information about Wiley products, visit our web site at www.wiley.com.

Library of Congress Cataloging-in-Publication Data is Available:

ISBN: 9781394424306 (Cloth)
ISBN: 9781394424313 (ePub)
ISBN: 9781394424320 (ePDF)

COVER DESIGN: PAUL MCCARTHY
AUTHOR PHOTOS: COURTESY OF THE AUTHORS

Printed and bound by CPI Group (UK) Ltd, Croydon, CR0 4YY
C9781394424306_250326

Contents

Designing for Humans, Not Machines

The Leader's Playbook: Shifting the
Human-Technology Power Dynamics

Introduction: Reflections from Mihir and Nancy

WE ARE PROBABLY an odd partnership as co-authors. On paper, we have little in common.

Nancy is a Chicago native and a Cubs fan, not a technologist by any stretch of the imagination, and a well-known CHRO who started her career in Silicon Valley when Mihir was 10 years old. She relies on humor to address all challenges, and her personal motto is, "If I can see the punchline, I can see the solution."

Mihir is an engineer by education, a successful CEO and a global thought leader. He immigrated to the US from India in 1995 and has been part of a few multi-billion-dollar business journeys in his career. In 2003, he co-founded Automation Anywhere, a company that invented two profound technological breakthroughs: Robotic Process Automation (RPA) and Agentic Process Automation (APA). Mihir's vision is a future in which human potential is unleashed through a partnership with AI agents.

Nancy and Mihir have worked together at Automation Anywhere since 2017. On Nancy's first day with the company, Mihir suggested that they co-author a book about radical change.

This is that book.

■　■　■

The book is structured around three parts:

- **Part I, The Exponential Era:** We will cover the incredible collision of forces today, where a combination of demographic decline, productivity stagnation, and the rise of artificial intelligence are combusting in a way that requires rapid transformation at a pace that rivals any in modern history. We propose that work wasn't always the way we define it today – it was made this way for another time, and it must change again. We will set the stage for the bold decision-making that is required for leaders to deliver accelerated outcomes in what we call The Five-Year Century.
- **Part II, The Four Illusions Holding Us Back:** Like any good story, there has to be an enemy. In this case, it's four illusions that have kept humanity from achieving its true potential for work: the illusions of incremental change, human-only work, hierarchical control, and technological servitude. We'll wrap each illusion with playbooks for leaders to conquer them.
- **Part III, Becoming Future-Ready:** In the final act, we will ensure leaders have the tools they need to succeed in The Five-Year Century. This includes developing strategies for outcomes-driven leadership, delivering on personalization, building trust, and ensuring everyone has the skills required to win in an AI-enabled world.

Our ultimate hope is that this book gives you the confidence to see how the best of humanity and technology can come together to make work – and the world – better for us all.

The Five-Year Century

PART

I

The Exponential Era

1

The Unparalleled Pace of Change

The Collapse of the Twin Engines of Growth

Even for those of us who have built careers and companies in Silicon Valley – a place where history tells us no transformation is too fast and no idea is too bold to start executing *today* – the sudden compression of time has hit with irreversible force.

We've worked in technology for decades – our whole careers. We've watched the internet transform commerce, mobile phones become computers, and cloud computing reshape how businesses operate. We invested in broadband well before anybody believed in it and we witnessed Netflix hunting for streaming technology eight years before their disruptive platform launched. We've seen transformations of all size and scale, across countless industries. However, we've never seen anything like what's happening now, with the simultaneous collision of multiple existential forces.

No one could have seen the pace of change happening this quickly in technology, demographics, and society.

For 150 years, the global economy has operated like a twin-engine plane. One engine represents population growth, with more workers entering the workforce each year. The other represents productivity growth, with each organization producing more value through better

3

tools, processes, and technology. When both engines hum, the plane soars. When one sputters, the other compensates to maintain altitude.

But what happens when one engine fails entirely while the other hasn't meaningfully improved in over a decade?

We're about to find out.

For the first time in modern history, the population engine has stalled. Demographic math is telling a story many organizations still haven't internalized – perhaps because the implications are hard to fathom. By 2030, every baby boomer will be over 65, traditionally considered retirement age. In the United States alone, roughly 11,200 people turned 65 every day during the "Peak 65" period from 2024 to 2026 – 11,200 experienced workers reaching retirement age, every single day.

At the same time, birth rates are plunging across the globe. The U.S. fertility rate fell to a record low of about 1.62 births per woman in 2023, far below the 2.1 required for population replacement.[1] Italy's rate hovers around 1.2, pointing to a sharply shrinking population without sustained immigration.[2] South Korea's fertility rate dropped to just 0.72 – the lowest in the world – creating demographic conditions so extreme that economists lack historical models to fully predict the consequences.[3]

By the mid-2030s, the world will have roughly 260–270 million people aged 80 and older, according to UN projections. With global births continuing to slow, the population at the very oldest ages will rival – and in some years exceed – the number of newborns for the first time in modern history. In practical terms, humanity is entering an era with more grandparents than babies, and it is arriving within little more than a decade.[4]

The United States reaches this tipping point sooner than most realize. Beginning around 2033, deaths are projected to exceed births, meaning that without immigration, the U.S. population would begin to shrink.[5] Population growth is expected to average just 0.2% annually from 2025 to 2055, compared with roughly 0.9% from 1975 to 2024.

Japan offers our preview of this future. Their workforce shortage cannot be solved solely through mobilization. Despite workforce participation reaching historic highs, Japan will face a shortage of 3.84 million workers by 2035 – nearly double the 2023 shortage.[6]

This means Japan's economy will have 3.84 million fewer workers than needed just eleven years from now, even if every available person joins the workforce.

Now look at the productivity engine – our supposed salvation. You'd think with all our technological advances, productivity would be soaring. For many individuals, it is. But for organizations across most sectors of the economy, productivity is stagnating, sometimes declining.

Labor productivity in U.S. manufacturing grew by 3.4% annually from 1987 to 2007. Then something broke. From 2010 to 2022, manufacturing productivity actually *declined* by 0.5%, in terms of measured growth rate over the period.[7] The fastest-growing manufacturing industries saw productivity drop from 6.5% annual growth to negative 0.6% over the same periods. These figures mark a historic reversal in the sector that once anchored America's industrial strength, despite unprecedented investments in digital technology, automation, and data infrastructure.

Recent research reveals that productivity gains are increasingly concentrated in a small number of tech-intensive sectors. From 2008 through the post-2020 period, only certain industries, such as computer systems design, online retail, and professional services, have pulled ahead. Traditional service businesses and trade sectors remain stagnant.[8] Despite trillions of dollars poured into IT spending, cloud computing, and digital transformation, the expected productivity revolution hasn't materialized across most of the economy.

If nothing changes, then the gross domestic product per capita growth in OECD (Organisation for Economic Co-operation and Development) countries is expected to fall from 1.0% annually (2006–2019) to 0.6% annually (2024–2060) – a 40% reduction driven entirely by aging populations and shrinking workforces.[9] This represents the largest demographically driven economic slowdown in modern history, affecting all developed economies simultaneously.

Here's what this means in practical terms. Historically, companies needed, on average, 5.1 people to generate $1 million in revenue. But what if in the future – because of a combination of technology acceleration and demographic shifts – they aimed to achieve $1 million of revenue with only three people? Where teams of 20 accomplished major projects in the past, what if only 12 were needed to deliver the same results? Can you imagine running your current operation with 40% fewer people? Because that type of operating model may be possible sooner than you expect.

Demographics and math are a big part of the road ahead. If your productivity doesn't increase dramatically, you can't maintain output as your workforce potentially shrinks. And if you cannot produce enough, you cannot support the welfare state that we have become used to, maintain infrastructure, and more. If you can't maintain output, you can't compete. What happens if you can't compete? Well, you know how that story ends.

Meanwhile, artificial intelligence and automation technologies are advancing at a pace that compresses decades of change into years, and years into months.

The pace of AI's expansion has become a lightning-speed sprint: GPUs are doubling in capability so fast that yesterday's state-of-the-art is outdated much faster. Data-center investment has exploded into the largest industrial build-out since the rise of the electrical grid, with hyperscalers pouring billions each month into power, cooling, and silicon just to keep up. Meanwhile, large language models are scaling by orders of magnitude, swallowing more parameters, modalities, and real-time data than any technology platform in history. The result is a compounding acceleration – each breakthrough in chips fuels bigger models, which demand larger data centers, which in turn make even more powerful models possible. We are no longer in an era of linear improvement; we are riding an exponential curve driven by AI.

At the time of writing in 2026, as stock markets continue to be anchored around the largest AI and technology companies driving historic multi-trillion valuations such as NVIDIA, Alphabet, Microsoft, Amazon, Apple, Meta, and Tesla, with upcoming blockbuster IPOs from OpenAI and Anthropic, many are questioning what the future will hold. Is there an AI bubble or will the multi-billion-dollar partnerships, deals, and investments that are made seemingly each day deliver the ROI that investors expect? Who owns the value: the builders of models, the owners of data, or the operators of outcome? How will AI reshape geopolitics at a time of accelerated social and political transformation?

No one yet fully understands the answers to these questions. But regardless of how things play out in the broader landscape in the coming years, we can't question the fact that AI is going to change the world and modes of working in ways that we can only imagine.

The twin-engine example – demographic decline meeting the technological acceleration driven by AI – creates what we call The Five-Year Century. It's one of the few times in history where there's an equal amount of excitement and anticipatory anxiety for what's ahead. Both sides are justified.

Traditional business cycles have always assumed gradual change. A company could spot a trend, study it, pilot a response, and scale deliberately. And while strategic decisions and investments will always require due diligence and thoughtfulness, there's no denying that the need for faster pivots and decision-making has arrived.

The mechanics of The Five-Year Century affect everything about how teams must operate. Skills that professionals spent decades mastering now have a much shorter shelf-life, down significantly from the 1980s. Strategic plans that once projected five years out now barely stretch across six months. The window for transformation has collapsed.

Despite this, most organizations still operate on industrial assumptions. They're trying to solve twenty-first century problems with nineteenth century thinking. They're digitizing bad processes instead of reimagining them. They're using revolutionary tools for evolutionary change.

At conferences, we often meet executives who think they're transforming their companies by moving to the cloud or upgrading their ERP (Enterprise Resource Planning) systems. They haven't grasped that the rules have changed. What got them here won't just fail to get them *there* – it will accelerate their decline.

What jobs will disappear, what jobs will grow, and what new categories will emerge? This question runs through the minds of people everywhere and is one we often get asked. It's an important question, but we think it's more important to look at a bigger picture question to assess where you stand: *Are you an AI optimist or an AI skeptic?*

For the AI optimist, these are the people who believe the current ideas are not all the ideas we have. The world is full of brilliant and creative people who have more ideas that can be dreamed of and turned into reality. Thus, more jobs will be created to solve new challenges and opportunities. At their core, the AI optimists believe the current version of the world is not the best world possible – they can always imagine something better and see how a once-in-a-multiple-generation technology can enhance lives for the better.

On the other side, there are the AI skeptics. These are the people who believe they have worked hard to fit into the current world. They believe the world may be changing too fast and it should work for them and their needs. They are nervous about the impact of AI on their careers and their jobs; they see AI as a technology that could one day displace them, so they are not going to embrace using it or learning how to apply it any more than they need to.

To be fair, neither of these views should be seen as right or wrong. They are two very real perspectives that people have across the world. Neither side should be too quick to judge; we are living in times of incredible transformation where we should seek to understand others' perspectives and learn from them.

No matter which camp you may sit in today – AI optimist or AI skeptic – our view is that it's undeniable that the transformation will change the nature of work to a large degree. AI has been invented and it cannot be un-invented. Individuals, companies, and countries are using it and will accelerate its usage to gain a competitive edge. It is better to embrace the world for what it is and shape it for what we want it to be versus what we wish it were.

The other truth is that work *has always adapted to society's needs*. As long as humans have needs that other humans can serve and resources to trade or share, there will always be work – this model should never go away.

To understand what the future of work might look like, especially in light of rapidly developing AI and declining populations, a better question might be: What will societies need in five years and how can AI best support it?

The demographic mathematics provide some answers – though they're not always rosy. As populations decline across developed nations, we can look to countries already facing these problems for a preview of what's to come.

This brings us to Japan – perhaps the first developed nation to wade into the storm of The Five-Year Century.

How the World Is Following in Japan's Footsteps

In a sparse apartment in a coastal Japanese city, an 80-year-old woman sat with her hands folded neatly in her lap. She was impeccably dressed, wearing a pressed white blouse, carefully styled silver hair, and a string of pearls that had belonged to her mother. But her eyes looked exhausted in a way that sleep couldn't fix.

"I was alone every day and feeling very lonely," she would later explain to authorities. "The first time I shoplifted was about 13 years ago. I wandered into a bookstore in town and stole a paperback novel."[10]

She paused, remembering that first arrest with something approaching fondness. "I was caught, taken to a police station, and questioned by the sweetest police officer. He was so kind. He listened to everything I wanted to say. I felt I was being heard for the first time in my life."[11]

Ms. N, as court documents identify her, had discovered something profound in that police station. She discovered visibility. After years of isolation following her husband's death, after watching friends disappear one by one, after her children moved to Tokyo for work and rarely called, she had found a perverse solution to her crushing loneliness.

Her neighborhood, once alive with the sounds of children playing and neighbors chatting, had grown eerily quiet. Many apartments stood empty, their windows dark and lifeless. The few remaining neighbors were also elderly, many too frail to socialize. The local school had closed years ago. The shopping street that once bustled with life now had more shuttered stores than open ones.

She began shoplifting deliberately, always selecting small items that were in full view of the security cameras. Each arrest brought human contact, conversation, and acknowledgment that she still existed. By the time authorities intervened, she had been arrested multiple times.

"The loneliness becomes physical," another elderly inmate at Tochigi Women's Prison explained. "It hurts here," she said, pressing a hand to her chest.

Inside the prison, these women found what they'd been desperately missing. They found three meals a day with other people, healthcare, daily human interaction, and most importantly, a sense that they existed.

"There are very good people in this prison," said Akiyo, 81, serving time at Tochigi. "Perhaps this life is the most stable for me."

Japan's prisons have been forced to adapt, essentially becoming nursing homes with steel bars. They've installed handrails in corridors, wheelchair ramps, and stocked adult diapers. Think about that for a moment. Japan has created a society where prison provides better care and community for the elderly than freedom.

What kind of economy are we building where prison becomes a retirement plan? Where isolation drives the elderly to commit petty crime for human contact?

Ms. N and Akiyo represent canaries in the coal mine of a global crisis. Elderly crime in Japan has nearly quadrupled over the past two decades. More than one in five arrests now involve seniors over 65, reaching 22.0% in 2019.[12] A Tokyo Metropolitan Government survey found that over half of elderly shoplifters lived alone, and 40% said they either didn't have family or rarely spoke with relatives.[13]

■   ■   ■

To understand why so many companies are stuck in failing patterns, we need to know their origins. Many of today's organizations were built for stability in an age of volatility. They were designed for control in a world that now demands radical creativity.

In the sixteenth century and earlier, work was intimate and self-directed. Most people labored alongside family or neighbors, setting their own pace and seeing projects through from start to finish. The rhythm of work was tied to the rhythm of life – rooted in community, autonomy, and craftsmanship. Many people were both specialists in their fields and generalists in business, as they had an area of expertise and also had to run their business. You might have been a farmer, but you also had to manage the business side of farming. Likewise, as a dressmaker, you were likely managing a budget sheet and attempting to attract more clients. Even as a sailor, you would not only receive a small wage, but you'd also receive an amount of equity in any profit. Work was personal, contextual, and human.

Then the Industrial Revolution transformed the way things were made while simultaneously redefining how humans thought about work. Strangers began working together at a massive scale. Tasks were broken down into repeatable parts. Workers became interchangeable. Standardization and efficiency became the highest virtues.

This approach created remarkable productivity. It enabled the mass production of goods that had once been luxury items, making them affordable to ordinary people. It raised living standards worldwide. And it was spectacularly successful.

The rise of the Industrial Age came with particular assumptions about how work should be organized.

First, hierarchy seemed natural and necessary, with someone at the top seeing the big picture while everyone else followed orders.

Second, standardization was believed to drive efficiency through finding the best way, documenting it, replicating it, and allowing no variations. Individual human differences? It doesn't matter.

Third, the belief emerged that humans serve the system, with the system's needs taking precedence and humans needing to adapt accordingly.

Fourth, change was viewed as linear and manageable, with tomorrow looking pretty much like today.

Finally, scale was thought to require control, with more people necessitating more rules, processes, and oversight. This is where you see companies require VP approval for a small expense purchase while risking millions on failed projects without question.

The ideas of the Industrial Age made perfect sense in their time. They created unprecedented wealth, lifted hundreds of millions out of poverty, and laid the foundation for the modern world – we owe an enormous debt of gratitude to that era.

Yet some of the age's underlying assumptions still shape the invisible operating system of today's businesses, so deeply embedded that we rarely question them. We continue to swim upstream even as industrial thinking increasingly holds us back in a world defined by AI and exponential technological advancement.

July 1831, Steele's Tavern, Virginia. Twenty-two year old Cyrus McCormick stood in a wheat field, about to demonstrate his mechanical reaper to local farmers.[14] After six weeks of work in his family's blacksmith shop, McCormick was convinced he had solved a problem that had stumped inventors for decades, including his own father.

The farmers crossed their arms and exchanged knowing glances as McCormick hitched a single horse to what looked like a bizarre hybrid of a sled, chariot, and farming tool. Imagine trying to explain this thing to your insurance company. "Well, it's part farm equipment, part medieval torture device, and it shakes a lot." The crowd must have thought this kid had lost his mind.

But it did work. In minutes, McCormick's machine harvested more wheat than a skilled man with a scythe could cut in an hour. One horse and one operator were doing the work that normally required an entire crew. The productivity gain was staggering, possibly a tenfold improvement.

Yet, when the demonstration ended, the farmers nodded politely, made small talk about the weather, and returned to their farms. They returned to the same scythes they'd been using their entire lives. They had just witnessed the future and chose to ignore it.

How could anyone standing in that Virginia field possibly envision that the vast majority of people would no longer need to farm? How could they imagine cities of millions, fed by the work of so few?

McCormick didn't give up, but progress was painfully slow. He sold one of his wheat reapers for nine years.[15] Sales trickled in during the 1840s, starting with two in 1841, seven in 1842, and twenty-nine in 1843.[16] However, by the time of the Civil War, his invention had transformed American agriculture. What seemed impossible in 1831 had become inevitable by 1861.

We face the same challenge today as the farmers watching McCormick's first demonstration. AI and automation serve as harbingers of a future where work itself undergoes complete reimagination. And like those farmers, we struggle to see beyond what we know.

Netflix is a popular example of a company staying ahead of the curve. In 1999, when broadband was still in its infancy, Netflix's founders were already exploring the potential of streaming technology. Nancy remembers from her venture capital days, sitting in on quarterly updates when Patty McCord from Netflix asked if she could attend. Why? Netflix was already looking for a company to acquire that would be in streaming. This was *eight years before* they'd launch streaming – they were barely a DVD mail business at that point. While everyone else thought they were focused on growing and perfecting those mailers, Netflix was hunting for the technology that would make those mailers obsolete. They didn't wait for time to force their decision. They dared to move.

The ability to see patterns early and the courage to act on them made all the difference. However, a similar company today would not have eight years to scale to launch, but about five months. Can you imagine your organization pivoting to a business model with unproven scale and nonexistent infrastructure, and launching successfully in five months? Probably not.

What are we missing?

■   ■   ■

The Industrial Age shaped our economies while simultaneously shaping our thought patterns. It created powerful illusions that once served us well but now constrain our ability to adapt. These illusions are so deeply embedded that they've become invisible to us.

The first illusion is the belief in incremental change. We believe the future will be a slightly better version of today. But we face discontinuous, exponential change that will render many current business models obsolete. What took decades now takes years, and what took years now takes months. We're living through a century of change compressed into five years: The Five-Year Century.

The second is the illusion of human-only work. We keep drawing arbitrary lines around "human work," even as AI continuously proves us wrong. Here's the question we should be asking: Instead of "What can AI do?" what if we asked, "Why should this be human work?"

Now, let's be clear: AI will transform jobs, and yes, eliminate some entirely. We're seeing it happen already. AI can perform tasks that previously employed thousands of humans. Roles we thought were safe may not be. The disruption is real, it's happening now, and we don't fully know how extensive it will be. No one knows exactly how this plays out. But the deeper truth could also be that AI exposes how much of what we labeled "human work" was never worthy of human potential in the first place.

The third illusion centers on hierarchical control. We assume transformation must cascade from the top down. However, profound changes often emerge from unexpected directions, particularly from younger generations who don't look for permission to innovate. In conversations with high school students, we tell them that the future of work could be like science fiction – where you talk to a computer and make a request, it pulls up applications, and AI agents dynamically get the work done in front of your eyes – in a way that is almost entertaining to watch. The students are never impressed by the explanation. Instead, they ask, "Well, how does work happen now? *Why don't you do it this way already?"*

Young people are accustomed to technology making things better, smarter, faster, easier, and more intuitive. So, what may feel like an AI disruption for many is common sense for them. In their eyes, AI makes things work how they should have always worked to begin with.

The fourth illusion concerns technological servitude. We've been conditioned to adapt to technology rather than designing technology that adapts to us. Our tools demand our compliance; we learn their menus, we adjust our workflows to fit their constraints, and increasingly we bend our working lives around the quirks of devices, apps, and platforms. How many passwords do you have? How many times have you cursed at your computer today?

What if the reverse were true? What if technology could learn your style, anticipate your needs, and handle the mundane so you can focus on the meaningful? What if technology served humans instead of the other way around?

The four illusions represent active barriers to survival, extending beyond simple intellectual errors. Everything changes once you see through them. The twin-engine plane of an expanding workforce and massive productivity gains doesn't have to die out mid-air and crash. Instead, today's challenges can be a launch pad for human potential.

The Industrial Age was built on standardization, with one-size-fits-all solutions optimized for efficiency and scale. But we're entering an age where personalization at scale becomes possible and necessary. In healthcare, we're transitioning from standardized treatments to personalized medicine based on an individual's genetic makeup.[17] In education, we're shifting from standardized curricula to customized learning paths. In entertainment and advertising, algorithms now curate individualized experiences.

Why should work be any different? Why should we continue organizing work in standardized ways when technology exists to create bespoke experiences tailored to individual strengths, preferences, and circumstances?

The Five-Year Century: The Choice Before Us

The pace of change continues to compress exponentially, moving beyond simple acceleration. This compression extends to human capability itself. The half-life of technical skills has collapsed to just 2.5 years, down from 10 to 15 years in the 1980s – an 83–85% reduction.[18] By 2030, 39% of workers' core skills will have fundamentally changed. Professionals must now reinvent themselves every two to three years just to remain relevant, compared to once or twice in an entire career a generation ago.

The path forward requires reimagining work, organizations, and how humans create value. Those who recognize the limitations of industrial thinking and adopt new mental models will have a significant advantage. Like Netflix in 1999, they'll see patterns forming before others do. They'll make bold moves while competitors hesitate. They'll reimagine their businesses for a world that doesn't yet exist but will soon.

We're helping to create the future here and now with every decision we make. But we're not in complete control of how it unfolds. AI is developing faster than our ability to understand its implications. The best we can do is to shape it thoughtfully while preparing for multiple scenarios.

The technologies emerging now offer opportunities to create more human-centered organizations where routine work is automated, decision-making is augmented, and humans are freed to apply their uniquely human capabilities to meaningful challenges.

Technology alone won't suffice to address these challenges. We need new ways of thinking. We need the courage to question assumptions about how work should be organized, how decisions should be made, and how value should be created.

Business leaders today are managing one of the most profound transitions in human history. We're going to make mistakes. Some pilots will fail. Some jobs will disappear forever. However, clinging to industrial models while the world transforms around us guarantees obsolescence for everyone.

Ms. N's story reveals what happens when systems designed for one kind of world persist in another. Her loneliness, her desperate search for connection, and her choice of prison over isolation indicate organizations and societies are operating on industrial assumptions.

In the pages ahead, we'll explore a promising new framework together. We'll shatter the illusions, embrace the possibilities, and grapple honestly with the challenges. We'll explore how to create organizations worthy of human potential while acknowledging the real cost of transformation.

Remember, as you read these words, the clock keeps ticking. Every minute you spend reading represents hundreds of AI agents created, dozens of processes automated, thousands of data points analyzed, and countless transactions processed.

The Five-Year Century waits for no one.

2

Why the Industrial Mind Won't Let Go

The Industrial Reprogramming of Human Work

In 1835, an eleven-year-old girl named Lucy Larcom walked through the gates of a textile mill in Lowell, Massachusetts. Her father had died. Her mother couldn't support eight children. So, Lucy became one of the first "Lowell Mill Girls" – young women mostly from New England farm families who would unknowingly become prototypes for the modern industrial worker.[1] The Lowell Mill Girls generally ranged from about 15–30 years old and were hired to spin and weave cotton cloth in huge brick factories during the Industrial Revolution.

Lucy's story matters because it illustrates how industrial thinking has reprogrammed human consciousness. Before the mills, work happened in rhythms – seasonal farming, craft production when orders came in, and rest when the work was done.[2] Her ancestors worked by the sun.

But Lucy worked by the bell.

Thirteen hours a day. Six days a week. Bells at 4:40 a.m. to wake. Bells at 5:00 a.m. to work. Bells for breakfast, lunch, and dinner. Bells to return. Bells to stop. The human body, which had evolved over millennia to respond to natural cycles, was forced to submit to mechanical time.[3,4]

17

Between tending machines, Lucy read voraciously, attended school part-time, and began publishing poems in *The Lowell Offering*, the mill girls' literary magazine. This exposure launched her reputation as a writer.

Here's what Lucy wrote years later about her experience in the mills: "I defied the machinery to make me its slave. Its incessant discords could not drown the music of my thoughts."[5]

These are beautiful words, but ultimately the machinery won. Lucy had to adapt. That's why she focused on reading and learning. She composed poems in her head while her hands worked the looms. She found ways to remain human inside the machine.

We can tell ourselves Lucy's story is history. But how many times have you picked up your phone today? How many notifications have you received for a meeting coming up? Do you schedule yourself in 15 minute blocks because 30 minutes feels like too much time to give?

We're all Lucy Larcom in some ways. We just have different bells.

■ ■ ■

Humans undergo a psychological rewiring in industrial-era systems. Pre-industrial humans worked in bursts – intense effort followed by rest.[6] However, the industrial systems demand consistent output, sometimes for up to 13 hours straight. No bursts. No rest. Just steady, mechanical production.

Mill workers initially rebelled. They organized some of the earliest women-led labor protests and unions in the U.S., striking over wage cuts and long hours. In 1834, when mill owners cut wages by 15%, Lucy's predecessors went on strike. "Union is power," they chanted. The strike failed. The owners had deep pockets, and the workers had families to feed.[7,8]

So, workers adapted through psychological compartmentalization. They learned to separate their "work self" from their "real self." They created mental escape routes like daydreaming, internal narratives, and secret resistance. Sound familiar? While Zoom meetings have transformed work in so many positive ways, how often do we find ourselves using them as a means to multi-task on PowerPoint or Outlook?

Too often, we are trying to do too much at once. This is also why too many of us commit to deadlines we know we can't meet but feel like we can't say no to.

This psychological split has become normalized. We are supposed to have "work-life balance" because the assumption is that work and life are opposing forces requiring balance. Before the Industrial Revolution, this concept would have been incomprehensible to a craftsperson. Their work was their life. Their life was their work. The idea that the two are separate came about during the Industrial Age. Traditional American corporations have long provided millions of people with stable jobs, pathways to upward mobility, and the chance to build meaningful careers that support their families. For generations, they have fueled an economy that's been a powerful engine of opportunity and innovation, creating environments where talent can grow and ambition can be rewarded. Despite these strengths, in recent years especially the nature of work has shifted in ways that blur the boundaries between professional and personal life. The rise of hybrid and remote work, global teams, and always-on communication has made it harder for many employees to protect their time, rest, and prioritize well-being. What once felt like flexibility can now feel like an unending workday, stretched across time zones and devices. Working from home can feel like living at work.

Even though the majority of people can sense that something is wrong with the way we work, positive change seems fleeting. To attract the workforce they need, businesses tout favorable perks and benefits – which employees often appreciate – but due to the industrial models we operate in, they often don't make the lasting impact they are intended to.

The End of the Interchangeable Worker

Frederick Winslow Taylor enters our story like a ghost, still haunting every workplace. Born in 1856 at the height of America's industrial ascent, Taylor was not a factory owner or tycoon. He was an engineer obsessed with efficiency, measurement, and control. At the turn of the twentieth century, as factories grew larger and more complex, Taylor set out to solve what he believed was industry's core problem: human inconsistency. His answer became known as *scientific management* – a system that promised to turn messy human labor into something predictable, optimizable, and scalable.

His time and motion studies at Bethlehem Steel increased productivity by 280% and fundamentally changed how we think about human capability.[9] He accomplished this by showing how to make human workers interchangeable.

Before Taylor, a craftsperson was irreplaceable. The skilled worker held deep knowledge in their minds about their trade and the muscle memory to execute the work flawlessly. After Taylor, any worker with the right tools could follow the "one best way." Knowledge moved from workers to management, the people who owned the tools and knew how to use them.[10]

In Taylor's schema, managers are at the top of a rigid pyramid, as they were believed to have the knowledge of how to do the work best. They impose the "how" onto the workers below them, who have no choice but to comply because all workplaces are the same, and the workers themselves are easily replaceable. That worked well in a different time. It is an entirely different world today in more than one way.

First, in today's environment, if you want something done the same way again and again – or even with minor adjustments – AI and automation can do that. We can no longer afford to have humans performing interchangeable work in this same way.

Second, the escape valves that once saved us from population decline are now sealed:

1. **An aging workforce** has a vast share of experienced managers and operators retiring at the same time. Between 2024 and 2026, approximately **11,200 Americans turn 65 every single day**, or more than **4 million people per year** reaching traditional retirement age.[11] This is not a temporary fluctuation; it is a demographic wave that has been building for decades. These exits represent the largest sustained loss of experienced talent in U.S. history, for example.

2. **Immigration** once provided fresh workers. Between 1880 and 1920, America absorbed 23 million immigrants. They powered the factories, built the railroads, and created industrial might.

Today? Large-scale immigration of this nature is improbable based on policy landscape, migration patterns, and math.

3. **Urbanization** unlocked a massive, one-time labor shift. In 1900, roughly 40% of Americans lived in cities. By 2000, that figure had reached nearly 80%. Tens of millions moved from farms into factories and offices, converting rural labor into industrial and service productivity. But this was a one-directional transformation. Once an economy is urbanized, there is no second wave. You cannot move people from farms to cities twice.

4. **Women entering the workforce** added massive capacity. Female participation rose from 34% in 1950 to 60% in 2000. Twenty-six percentage points of additional workers. But again – a one-time boost. We can't add women to the workforce twice. Although there is a chance of improvement here, it is nowhere close to what we have done before.[12]

We're trying to run a twentieth century economy with twenty-first century demographics. We need a 40% productivity gain just to maintain our current economic output. It won't come from more people working, nor will it come from more or better technology alone. It can only emerge from a fundamentally reimagined partnership between humans and technology – one that finally breaks free from Taylor's interchangeable worker and restores humans to the role they were never meant to abandon: judgment, creativity, and decision-making at the center of economic value.

The Generation That Collapsed the Adoption Curve

Technology adoption curves were designed by Baby Boomers, for Baby Boomers. The most widely accepted adoption model assumes slow initial adoption by early adopters (2.5%), gradual acceptance by the early majority (13.5%), followed by mainstream adoption over several years, even decades. Anyone who has read *Crossing the Chasm* by Geoffrey Moore understands how reliably predictable these adoption curves can be and how important they are to understanding the spread of disruptive technologies. Moore shows how innovations move in distinct waves – from early enthusiasts to the pragmatic majority – and why so many breakthroughs fail at the moment they attempt to leap between those two worlds. These curves have remained relatively unchanged for three generations, making them appear to be permanent laws of marketing rather than time and context-bound charts.

This isn't true, however. Gen Z broke all of the models for predicting technology adoption. They don't have early adopters because they're *all* early adopters. They don't gradually accept technology – they inhale it. TikTok reached a billion users in four years. ChatGPT hit 100 million users in two months. Professors and teachers are encouraging students to use LLMs because so many students will use them whether or not they are told. They grew up using iPads in school instead of books in many cases – asking an LLM to find them answers is as natural to them as breathing.

Venmo didn't "diffuse" through Gen Z the way credit cards once moved through previous generations. It became a default infrastructure almost overnight. In many college communities, paying with cash is now anomalous. The technology didn't cross a chasm – it simply appeared fully formed as social plumbing.

In comparison, companies and organizations have been slow to adopt many of these same prevalent technologies. By the time corporations form a committee to study a new technology, Gen Z has already adopted it and moved on to the next thing.

The industrial deal was straightforward: trade time for financial security. Work hard, climb the ladder, and retire with a pension. Social Security and Medicare will cover the gaps as you get older. These bargains are dead, but we as a society continue to pretend they exist.

Job tenure hasn't actually changed much (the median is still around four years in a role), but the psychological contract between employees and employers has been shattered.[13] Young workers aren't fooled. They watched their parents give decades to a company only to be laid off when the winds of change blew. Loyalty in the modern era has not been rewarded. This was a tough blow to many Baby Boomers, but younger generations have come to expect this treatment. They've come of age during the 2008 Recession, the COVID-19 pandemic and in the age of AI. They've never known employment security, and so they don't expect it. Ask a Gen Z employee to go above and beyond, and they have the audacity to ask for either more compensation or PTO to make up for it.

But is it audacity? Or is it a natural response to their economic situation?

Look at their reality:

- Real wages are down 5.5% since 1975 for under-35 workers
- Home prices are up 40% relative to income
- Student debt averages $30,000 per graduate
- Life expectancy is up 50% which is great, but you still need to fund those extra years
- The average retirement age has gone up three years since the 1990s.[14,15,16]

Gen Z is redefining the relationship between life and work in a way that stands out from previous generations. Having grown up in an era shaped by economic uncertainty and rapid technological change, they place a higher premium on balance and boundaries. This doesn't mean they're less ambitious – only that they expect ambition to coexist with a sustainable and fulfilling life outside the office.

And yet, those who should be best suited to reinvent the way they work – including those within Gen Z – still cling to industrial thinking across many facets of their daily work.

The pandemic provided a natural experiment in work design. Suddenly, every assumption about "how work must be done" was tested simultaneously. The results could have shattered industrial thinking forever.

Productivity went up for a while. Workers spent less time commuting (the average American commutes 27.6 minutes each way), less time in meetings (down 12%), more time actually working, *and* more time living. Kids saw their parents during the day. People ate lunch with their families.

While there is no denying the culture, creativity, and collaboration that come from being together in person – and many leaders see real value in bringing teams back into the office – the two-year global experiment in remote work proved something equally important: there is no longer a one-size-fits-all model for how work gets done. The future is not strictly office-first or home-first but can be intentionally hybrid. That is why so many organizations are now designing flexible operating models that blend in-person connection for chunks of the week with virtual work on remaining days, allowing teams to capture the energy of co-location without sacrificing the flexibility that working days at home can enable. The precise balance will differ by role and by company, but there is validation that many employees have demonstrated they can be productive with a mix of working in the office and at home.

Yet despite the many positive shifts in ways of working that the pandemic brought about, there are still many that we haven't shaken. Why? Because of a phenomenon called "path dependence."

Path dependence is economics-speak for "We do it this way because we've always done it this way." However, it's more insidious than a simple force of habit. Every system, process, and structure in modern organizations is based on industrial thinking. Changing one piece requires changing everything.

Consider the simple act of hiring. The entire process assumes industrial logic:

- Job descriptions list tasks, not problems to solve.
- Resumes lead with experiences spent in years completing activities, and only the best ones demonstrate the value created with results.
- Interviews happen during "business hours" (an industrial concept).
- Salaries are often based on "experience" (which really means "time spent"), not always on contribution.

To truly change hiring, you'd need to reimagine job design, compensation, performance measurement, team structure, and legal frameworks. Each depends on the others. All assume industrial thinking. It's easier to perpetuate dysfunction than untangle the web.

This begs the question: What progress did we make during the Information Age? Of course, we made a significant amount. But for every two technological steps forward between 2000 and 2025, there has been one step taken back.

Most "digital transformation" efforts just put broken processes on laptops and smartphones. We didn't reimagine work; we gave it a user interface. We often digitized dysfunction. As Peter Drucker said, "There is nothing so useless as doing efficiently that which should not be done at all." Put in other words, efficiency is meaningless if you're optimizing the *wrong work*. Because we haven't updated our thinking, technological advances like AI may simply amplify industrial models.

■ ■ ■

Fish in the deep sea don't notice the water around them because they've never experienced its absence. We don't see industrial thinking for the same reason. It's the only model most of us have known, and it shapes our lives from our school days to our work lives, until we finally retire.

But here's what's changing: The generations now entering the workforce have experienced something different. They've seen remote work succeed (if not remote school). They've used AI to amplify their capabilities. They've built businesses from bedrooms. They know alternatives exist.

Industrial thinking will eventually come to an end; the demographics guarantee it. Technology enables it. Young workers demand it. The question is whether your organization will lead the transition or become a casualty.

This is a unique moment in time. For the first time in 200 years, we can organize human effort without the constraints of industrial models. We have tools that make geography irrelevant. We have AI that can handle routine, process-driven work, and adapt and learn within reason. We have communication systems that make hierarchies unnecessary – and technology that requires flatter organizational models. We have everything we need to build something better on the success of the generations who came before us.

Yet, we hesitate. We cling to Lucy Larcom's bells, just dressed up as calendar notifications. We maintain Taylor's separation of thinking and doing, just with corporate titles that align to functional expertise but not business outcomes. We preserve industrial logic with better graphics.

We cling to the past today because letting go requires taking a bold stance and acknowledging much of what we call "management" is unnecessary. It requires re-imagining organizations and work itself around outcomes rather than departments, functions, or standard job titles. Most of all, letting go of industrial thinking requires seeing it for what it is. You can't build the future while living in the past.

The Industrial Age brought us incredible prosperity. It lifted millions from poverty. It created the modern world. It gave us mass production and affordable goods, railroads and global shipping, modern banking, and the rise of a broad middle class. It accelerated advances in medicine and public health, dramatically extending life expectancy. It fostered education, built the infrastructure of modern cities, and connected people, markets, and ideas at a scale humanity had never seen before. It's something to be celebrated in the tales of history.

But the Industrial Age is over and that's not a bad thing.

Work hasn't always looked the way it does today. It became this way for a reason in a different world, and it can and must change again.

Can you envision something different and something better?

3

Paying More for Less

A Healthcare System Caught in the Twin-Engine Problem

In May 2022, one of the largest publicly traded healthcare systems in the United States – a multi-billion-dollar hospital and ambulatory care operator – faced a crisis that no balance sheet could repair. After two years of unrelenting pandemic pressure, the organization hemorrhaged 5,800 nurses *in a single quarter.*[1] The departures weren't simply about wages; they were driven by exhaustion, burnout, and a belief among many nurses that the system no longer gave them the time, support, or staffing to adequately care for patients.

In response, the healthcare system's leadership reached for a familiar corporate lever: spending. They rolled out sign-on bonuses of up to $25,000, expanded retention incentives, and added shift differentials that rivaled Wall Street overtime. They more than doubled their spending on contract labor – $370 million, up from $185 million the year before – just to keep hospital floors open.[2]

In other words, the healthcare system ended up paying *twice as much for the same work,* while still failing to address the core issue – an exhausted workforce that needed better systems, better tools, and better working conditions, not just bigger checks.

The result led to operating margins collapsing from 18.4% to 14.1% despite revenue growth. The organization was making more money but keeping less of it. Their financial headache was broadly a symptom of our twin-engine plane problem. Let's start with productivity – specifically, their HR systems.

The average cost of replacing a single nurse is now estimated at $90,000 per position – the financial equivalent of setting a premium luxury vehicle on fire every time someone quits.[3] And even after absorbing that loss, hospitals wait three to six months to fill the vacancy, during which the remaining nurses perform the work of two people for the pay of one.[4] For the healthcare system we're referencing, the situation was even more punishing: contract nurses cost two to three times more than permanent staff, meaning every departure triggered not just operational pain but an escalating financial spiral.[5]

But the workforce crisis wasn't just an HR failure – it was a pipeline failure. In 2021 alone, U.S. nursing schools turned away over 90,000 qualified applicants because they didn't have enough faculty.[6] That's an entire city's worth of people who *wanted* to become nurses, were qualified to become nurses, and were ready to enter the workforce – yet the healthcare system had no capacity to train them. The organization wasn't just losing nurses faster than they could hire them; the entire national supply chain of new nurses was bottlenecked.

Eventually, the system's hiring pool dried up. With costs rising, vacancies unfilled, and no sustainable pipeline in sight, the organization began selling hospitals in 2024 just to reduce debt and stabilize its balance sheet.

Why did traditional approaches fail? Because each decision made sense in isolation – bonuses, travel nurses, retention incentives – but together, they accelerated the collapse. They applied Industrial Age solutions to Five-Year Century problems, trying to purchase their way out of a systemic failure that required redesigned processes, smarter automation, and improved working conditions, not larger checks.

How Information Democratization Broke the Industrial Playbook

Fifty years ago, a nurse in one city had no idea what nurses across the state were making. They couldn't compare benefits packages across hospitals. They couldn't text their nursing school classmates working in other healthcare systems to ask about working conditions. They certainly couldn't read online forums about which hospitals to avoid.

Information scarcity created employer power. If you worked at a healthcare system in 1975 and they offered you a $2,000 raise, you took it. You had no framework to evaluate whether that was fair. You didn't know whether the hospital across town was offering $5,000 raises, better shifts, and more flexibility. Your information came from your employer and your closest peers.

The Industrial Age thrived on an information monopoly, which proved highly effective. This allowed companies to maintain institutional knowledge and customer relationships, as employees – like a nurse working on the same floor for 30 years – rarely left. This stability ensured consistent revenue, controlled costs (especially replacement costs, as training was a one-time investment), and manageable risks. Culture was also easier to control due to long-lasting relationships, fostering loyalty that was safeguarded by the perceived impossibility of leaving due to information scarcity. Workers, with limited options and awareness of alternatives, tolerated conditions that would be unacceptable today, enabling management to demand more and offer less.

However, the advent of the internet shattered this monopoly. Suddenly, nurses and workers everywhere had access to a wealth of information – job openings, salaries, reviews, and stories of both success and failure. This democratization of information didn't just level the playing field; it completely upended the entire game.

The healthcare system in reference tried to solve an Information-Age problem with Industrial-Age solutions. More money? Nurses could calculate exactly how much more they'd make as traveling nurses. Retention bonuses? They could see which hospitals didn't require golden handcuffs to keep staff. Sign-on bonuses? Every nurse knew these were desperation moves by struggling hospitals.

The information asymmetry that made industrial management possible had evaporated.

When "Best Practices" Fail

What makes the healthcare system story instructive is that the company wasn't using outdated approaches. They were using what every consultant, every MBA program, and every leadership book would recommend: competitive compensation, retention bonuses, recruitment incentives, and market-based solutions to market-based problems.

In business today, CEOs and upper management are typically responsible for driving outcomes across four areas which we will look at across various case studies in the book: revenue growth, cost reduction, risk management, and culture. The healthcare system's conventional responses unfortunately didn't succeed in any of the four.

Revenue: Growth Is Capped When a Workforce Can't Meet System Demands

At its core, leadership is accountable for driving top-line growth. Traditional logic says, "Maximize output from existing resources, push harder, optimize utilization, and squeeze more from less."

But this approach breaks down when the workforce is shrinking, burned out, or leaving altogether. The healthcare system attempted to hire aggressively, and revenue did increase. But revenue could not outrun the significant cost escalation. It was like pouring water into a bucket with a widening hole – and paying double for each gallon.

Their revenue strategy collided directly with the second responsibility: cost reduction.

Cost: Optimizing Unit Costs While Ignoring System Costs Is a Losing Game

The cost paradigm has fundamentally shifted. You can no longer solve operational problems simply by adding more labor, the way you might add more servers to a data center. Industrial Age thinking focuses on lowering hourly wages, minimizing benefits, and reducing training – optimizing the *unit cost* of labor.

But in complex human systems, unit cost thinking often creates massive *system* costs.

The healthcare system's decision to suppress nurse wages didn't lower costs; it triggered an exodus that doubled contract labor expenses. Their underinvestment in training didn't improve efficiency; it accelerated knowledge loss, with each departure costing an estimated

$90,000.[7] When leaders treat people as inputs to keep the machine running, rather than designing systems that keep people supported and productive, costs expand in every direction.

Risk: When Controls Become Risks, Organizations Lose Sight of Reality

Many leaders believe they can address revenue and cost challenges first, then get to risk. In The Five-Year Century, that sequencing doesn't work. Risk levels are structurally higher, and traditional mitigation approaches often create the very vulnerabilities they intend to prevent.

Industrial Age risk management builds layers of controls – more approvals, more procedures, more audits. But when these systems consume so much attention that they blind you to external signals, your risk systems become the risk themselves.

The healthcare system faced this. The market had been signaling a nurse shortage for more than a year, yet the organization continued operating as if its historical stability made it immune. Risk was assumed to be static, when in reality it was compounding. In The Five-Year Century, the privilege of slow correction simply doesn't exist.

Culture: When People Have Options, They Are Not Afraid to Move On

Culture is often described as intangible, but it is a direct outcome of how organizations operate. Industrial Age culture-building relied on hierarchy, rules, and compliance. Today, workers have full visibility: they know what other organizations pay, what conditions are better, and where they are valued.

The result is simple: if culture doesn't support people, they look elsewhere.

And leaders still must use their authority to protect culture at the macro level. A high-velocity operating environment cannot tolerate individuals who resist necessary organizational evolution. The margin for error has collapsed; agility is now a survival trait.

At the healthcare system, cultural erosion wasn't caused by attitudes. It was caused by math: understaffing led to overwork, which led to turnover, which led to knowledge loss, which led to lower productivity – creating a competitive disadvantage that made talent attraction even harder.

The nursing education bottleneck makes this crystal clear. Why couldn't nursing schools find faculty? Experienced nurses can make far more money in clinical practice than in teaching. The traditional solution would be to increase faculty salaries. But schools can't afford to match hospital salaries. So, the shortage continues.

What if AI and automation could handle the routine parts of nursing education? What if virtual reality could provide clinical experience? What if we could amplify the impact of one expert instructor to teach thousands, rather than just dozens?

To answer those questions would require abandoning our assumptions about how education and other centuries-old systems work.

■　■　■

If the last decade has taught leaders anything, it is this: organizations rarely fail because the path forward is invisible – they fail because the familiar path feels safer than the unfamiliar one. Familiar dysfunction becomes its own comfort zone. Leaders can predict its failures, budget for its inefficiencies, and navigate around its faults. The dysfunction is costly, but at least it is *legible*.

This is why Industrial Age operating models persist long after their usefulness has evaporated. They provide an illusion of control in a world that no longer behaves predictably. Take performance management. Most systems still in use today trace directly back to World War II frameworks built for 19-year-old soldiers entering combat. Yet modern businesses continue using those same structures to evaluate mid-career professionals with mortgages, specialized expertise, and decades of institutional knowledge. Everyone knows the system is mismatched, but because it's familiar – and the alternatives feel uncertain – organizations cling to it. The core psychological trap is we overweight the risks of changing a broken system and underweight the risks of keeping it.

This brings us to the real challenge: most leaders are not trapped by a lack of technology, tools, or talent. They are trapped by a set of inherited illusions – beliefs that once ensured success but now distort reality. These illusions shape how leaders perceive revenue, cost, risk, and culture. They color every decision, every priority, and every trade-off. And if left unexamined, they guarantee that familiar dysfunction becomes permanent failure.

The chapters ahead break down the four Industrial Age illusions that quietly sabotage progress in The Five-Year Century – revealing why they persist, how they mislead even the most experienced leaders, and what it takes to dismantle them before they hinder the growth of your organization.

Your next move matters most because it is the moment you choose whether to remain inside those illusions or step beyond them.

PART

II

The Four Illusions
Holding Us Back

4

The Illusion of Incremental Change

Why Humans Misread Exponential Change

It's surprising to think about, but workplace productivity hasn't meaningfully improved since 2008. Despite the iPhone, cloud computing, social media, collaboration tools, and trillions of dollars poured into digital transformation, it still takes about five people to produce $1 million in economic output – the same ratio as the flip phone era. From 2010 onward, U.S. labor productivity grew at an anemic 0.8% annually, far below the historical average of 2.1% since 1947.[1]

Yet during this same period, global spending on information technology consistently ran into the multi-trillion-dollar range each year, reaching more than $4–5 trillion annually by the early 2020s and continuing to climb.[2] Over more than a decade, that adds up to tens of trillions of dollars invested in software, hardware, cloud infrastructure, and digital transformation initiatives worldwide. Some outcomes have improved, but the environment also has become more complex, fragmented, and cognitively demanding. Instead of accelerating productivity, new tools often created parallel systems, extra steps, and additional layers of work. The net result: The productivity needle hasn't moved as much as we'd expect.

If companies continue to rely on incremental improvements, growth will stall – and societies dependent on rising productivity to fund social programs will face unsustainable pressure. Incrementalism has become a liability. The comfortable belief that a company can drift forward with 3–5% annual improvements is a path toward irrelevance. The world now changes exponentially, yet organizations plan linearly. Annual planning cycles assume tomorrow will be a slightly modified version of today. However, the math of the modern world no longer supports that assumption.

Shifting away from incremental thinking will be uncomfortable. Exponential futures feel unrealistic because our brains are wired to extrapolate from what we already know. But when organizations commit to step-change productivity, the impact on people, culture, and performance can be transformative. To see this in practice, let's take a look at an example from Brazil.

■ ■ ■

In 2023, one of South America's largest energy companies with 45,000 employees – and a company that underpins Brazil's energy security, fiscal stability, and export economy – hit a wall that traditional planning couldn't overcome.

With more than $50 billion in annual tax obligations as a multinational company, every tax season the same ritual played out. Starting in January, the tax team began working weekends. By February, they were pulling all-nighters. By March, the office was their primary home. Brazil's tax regime – spread across an estimated hundreds of thousands of pages of laws, decrees, and constantly changing regulations – had grown beyond human comprehension. Many leaders running global businesses say it's one of the most complicated tax environments in the world.

The human cost was enormous. Each new tax regulation added to a stack that no one – and certainly no team – could fully grasp. Professionals with advanced degrees spent months manually cross-referencing regulations, checking calculations, and searching for compliance issues. They were drowning in complexity, and each year the water rose higher.

The irony cut deep. The Brazilian energy company used cutting-edge technology for deepwater oil exploration, pushing the boundaries of what was possible 7,000 feet below the ocean surface. Yet in their offices, humans were doing work that humans were never meant to do. The same company that could find oil deposits miles beneath the Atlantic couldn't find a way to calculate taxes without hindering their employees' morale – and sleep schedules.

However, the company's CIO and his team were able to see what others missed. While their peers focused on marginal improvements, they recognized that the entire premise was wrong. Calculating taxes was inhuman. The question wasn't how to do it faster, but whether humans should do it at all.

Tax calculation is just one example in a long history of humans asking humans to solve problems machines are better suited for. This is not because tax work lacks sophistication – on the contrary, tax professionals operate at the intersection of law, finance, and regulatory judgment – but because the mechanical act of large-scale tax calculation itself is a machine problem.

This pattern repeats across centuries.

The printing press revolution of the 1440s offers a parallel. In medieval Europe, books were so valuable that libraries chained them to desks. European scribes could produce maybe one book per year. Knowledge moved at the speed of handwriting.

When Johannes Gutenberg introduced his printing press, the response was predictable. A goldsmith by trade and inventor by obsession, Gutenberg combined movable metal type with a mechanical press to industrialize the written word for the first time in history. Johannes Trithemius, a learned monk, dismissed these printed books as "deficient" compared to hand-copied manuscripts.[3] The Parisian scribes didn't just criticize – they physically attacked printing presses in 1476.[4] They feared a loss of craftsmanship and, correctly, a loss of their jobs.

But by 1500, nine million printed volumes circulated in Europe – which added fuel for the Reformation, the Scientific Revolution, and the Enlightenment. The scribes focused on preserving the old way. Gutenberg focused on enabling a new world.[5,6,7]

Four hundred years later, the pattern repeated with railroads. In 1830, the United States had exactly 14 miles of railroad track. Canal operators, who moved cargo at 4 mph, saw no threat in these experimental contraptions. They had thousands of miles of proven waterways, established routes, and steady profits. What could trains on rails offer that boats on water couldn't?

The Illinois & Michigan Canal opened in 1848, a marvel of engineering that became obsolete soon after it opened.[8] By 1860, America had 30,000 miles of railroad track.[9] Railroads didn't just move goods faster – they collapsed geographic distance, synchronized national markets for the first time, and made entirely new industries possible. Moreover, trains moved at 20 mph at $1/10^{th}$ the cost per ton-mile of canals.

The pattern never changes: exponential change arrives disguised as an experiment. Linear thinkers optimize the old way, adding incremental improvements to dying systems. By the time the old guard notices the threat, the curve has already taken off.

Our brains evolved for a world where almost nothing changed quickly. As Peter Diamandis describes, humans lived in "local and linear" ecosystems for millions of years. Harvests, populations, and technologies shifted gradually; nothing doubled overnight.[10]

Researchers call our default mode Exponential Growth Bias (EGB) – the universal tendency to underestimate exponential processes.[11] Studies show that when predicting exponential outcomes, people are not just off by a little – they are consistently off by orders of magnitude.

Neuroscience reveals the problem. Your intraparietal sulcus – the brain region for numerical processing – needs serious prefrontal cortex support to handle exponential reasoning.[12] That prefrontal cortex doesn't fully develop until your mid-twenties, and even then, it struggles with exponential math. But individual cognitive limitations are just the beginning. We've institutionalized our linear thinking into every organizational structure, turning organizational blind spots into systemic failures.

We've even institutionalized our resistance to change. Psychological research has shown that humans tend to overvalue what they have and undervalue what they *could* have. Loss aversion (the name for this cognitive bias) is twice as powerful as gain motivation.[13] As such, most risk management frameworks kill the potential for moonshots.

To make this concrete, consider two fictional companies:

Linear Growth Company – Year 1

Q1: $10M
Q2: $11M
Q3: $12M
Q4: $14M

Exponential Growth Company – Year 1

Q1: $0.3M
Q2: $0.6M
Q3: $1.2M
Q4: $2.4M

Early on, the exponential curve looks unimpressive. But by Year 2:

Linear Growth Company – Year 2

Q1: $15M
Q2: $16M
Q3: $18M
Q4: $21M

Exponential Growth Company – Year 2

Q1: $4.8M
Q2: $9.6M
Q3: $19.2M
Q4: $38.4M

Within another year, exponential growth surpasses $0.5 billion per quarter. Linear systems, no matter how optimized, never catch up.

The problem isn't intelligence. It's imagination trapped inside a linear frame. When you can only see straight lines, every curve looks like a cliff.

What Happens When You Try Something Exponential

How hard is it to think exponentially? Try answering these without calculating:

Question 1: If AI capability improves 10% monthly, how much better is it after 24 months?

- **Linear thinking says:** 2.4× better (10% × 24 months)
- **Exponential reality:** nearly 10× better (1.1^{24})

Question 2: If an AI product has 100 million users and user adoption grows at 8% per month, how long until it reaches 1 billion users?

- **Linear thinking says:** more than 9 years (900 million ÷ ~8 million net new users per month)
- **Exponential reality:** about 32 months (100 million × $1.08^{32} \approx$ 1 billion)

If you missed them, you're not alone. What matters is not knowing the math – it's knowing that your instincts will be wrong when the stakes are high.

Which brings us back to the Brazilian energy company example from earlier.

Their leaders reframed the core question:

> **Stop asking, "How do we do the same work with fewer people?"**
> **Start asking, "How do we 10× the output per person?"**

Traditional thinking treats work as fixed and people as the variable. Exponential thinking treats people as fixed and methods as the variable. This shift unlocked their big breakthrough.

■ ■ ■

When the Brazilian energy company's leadership made this mental shift, they stopped seeing AI as a tool to help humans work faster. They saw it as a way to do work humans should never have done in the first place. Calculating taxes across hundreds of thousands of pages of continuously evolving regulations is not merely difficult – it is a scale, speed, and precision problem that traditional human workflows were never designed to handle.

The transformation began with an experiment. Instead of another incremental improvement, the organization fed Brazil's entire tax code into an AI model. The AI didn't need to understand the tax code the way humans do, parsing meaning from dense legal language. It needed to recognize patterns and apply rules, something AI does infinitely better than humans. Its advantage was brute-force pattern recognition, rules execution at machine speed, and perfect consistency – all applied across a regulatory system too vast for any human team to reliably maintain.

The result?

The AI system found $120 million in tax savings in three weeks.[14]

Not three years. Not three quarters. *Three weeks.*

The savings came from errors and optimizations that humans had overlooked for years – not through incompetence, but due to the limitations of human cognition. The AI could hold hundreds of thousands of pages in its "mind" simultaneously, cross-reference millions of transactions against thousands of rules, and identify patterns invisible to even the most experienced tax professionals. It uncovered legitimate deductions hidden in obscure regulations, identified filing optimizations across various tax jurisdictions, and exposed errors that had been replicated year after year because no human could process enough information to spot them.

But the financial gain wasn't the most important breakthrough.

With the $120 million of tax savings in mind, the company was able to consider objectives to reinvest into renewable energy and strategic projects to further long-term growth. The example demonstrates how a tax department – a cost center previously constrained by manual scale and regulatory burden – could theoretically become a strategic engine driving innovation, sustainability, and culture change.[15]

The energy company's transformation demonstrates how exponential thinking simultaneously transforms all four leadership responsibilities. While revenue didn't increase directly from this example, the organization did save $120 million in tax payments that increased its cash capital to invest in new areas – theoretically those it felt would be able to increase its topline growth. Cost went down as the company paid less tax, and the need for overtime and weekend work went away. Risk management improved because AI doesn't make tired mistakes at 2 a.m. during tax season. What about culture? For the first time in 15 years, the tax team had lives outside the office. Employees who had been bogged down in spreadsheets were freed to focus on more strategic work – analyzing the tax implications of new ventures, optimizing corporate structures for tax efficiency, and collaborating with business units on growth initiatives. With the support of AI, the same talented people – freed from overly manual work – became exponentially more valuable.

■   ■   ■

We are living in an era that is both exhilarating and, at times, unnerving; whatever AI capabilities you see today represent the least powerful they will ever be. We are only on the one-yard line for what's ahead.

Like the first iPhone, which couldn't copy and paste, or the first ChatGPT release, which had difficulty remembering previous conversations, what seems impressive now will look primitive in a short time.

NVIDIA now releases new generations of AI chips on a near-annual cadence, delivering step-change gains in performance and efficiency; LLM models like OpenAI's ChatGPT, Anthropic's Claude, and Google's Gemini are being trained and enhanced at breakneck pace; and at Automation Anywhere, within six months our own process models moved from 30% completion to up to 90% automated process completion – significantly faster than the three years we had projected.

Capabilities that were research experiments just two years ago – real-time video generation, autonomous agents, multimodal reasoning – are now moving into production across finance, healthcare, manufacturing, and customer service, beginning to transform entire categories of routine knowledge work.

Despite the rapid advancement, linear thinkers may still see current limitations and dismiss the technology. "It makes mistakes," they say about AI. "It can't do everything a human can do. It hallucinates." They're evaluating a technology that improves exponentially using criteria designed for things that improve incrementally.

In late 2022, generative AI was largely viewed as a technology that wasn't yet ready for mass adoption – despite the excitement building around it. Within 24 months, it became embedded in search engines, productivity software, software development, customer support, marketing, finance, and healthcare. ChatGPT went from zero to 100 million users in two months – and as of this writing, over 800 million people use it weekly (10% of the world's population) and its adoption is continually increasing, along with the rate of adoption from its competitors from Google, Anthropic, Meta, and beyond.

We've crossed into a world where things happen faster than expected, not slower. We used to live in a world where everything took longer than expected. That's the world we all come from.

Suddenly, we are living in a Five-Year Century where everything takes *less* time than expected. In this compressed timeframe, a 6-12 month head start can equal an insurmountable advantage over your competitors. So why aren't large enterprises moving faster to transform?

The irony is hard to miss: many of the largest, most successful organizations are unfortunately often the slowest to adopt AI at scale. Their success and carefully engineered processes – which can be advantages in many areas – can become anchors that slow self-disruption. They are often optimized to protect what works, not to reinvent what might render it obsolete. However, when the cost of inaction is visible and immediate, complexity becomes a catalyst rather than an excuse.

The Brazilian energy company demonstrated that even the most complex, regulated, and traditionally human-intensive work can be transformed exponentially and lead to accelerated outcomes. If AI can navigate Brazilian tax code – some of the most complicated regulations on Earth – what can't it handle for your team?

The Leader's Playbook: Fostering Exponential Thinking

1. Start with Pain, Not Strategy

Forget Simon Sinek's *Start with Why* for a moment. Instead, *start with pain*. What is the operational challenge that's hindering team value and human potential? For one organization, tax season was an example. For your organization, it might be customer service backlogs that result in millions of dollars in lost revenue, contract reviews that delay deals for weeks, or talent recruitment processes that take so long that the best candidates accept other offers – or worse, go to your competitors.

Whatever keeps you up at night – that's your exponential opportunity. Pain points are signals indicating where exponential solutions will have the greatest impact. The worse the pain, the greater the potential transformation.

2. Have an Autonomous Enterprise Mindset

The autonomous enterprise is possible: Where up to 80% of work can be fully automated or AI-assisted, enabling people to focus on what matters most. To get there, you need to think big from the start: *Challenge each department or team with a 20% autonomous goal.*

Don't ask where AI can help. This will take you on a path where AI is bolt-on to current work. This generally doesn't lead to success. Instead, ask where humans need involvement. This is what an autonomous enterprise is all about. Turning the question around leads you to a very different answer.

You can ask leaders to provide funding with some ROI projections before you start, but you shouldn't get bogged down with a detailed ROI plan at the beginning. Traditional budget processes kill exponential innovations because they demand linear proof for exponential possibilities. Today's best organizations give teams permission to fail fast and learn faster. The lessons from failed AI-first transformation attempts are often more valuable than marginal successes because they reveal which work requires human intelligence and which is just human habit.

You'll likely find that tax calculation isn't the only complex, manual work hiding in your organization. Procurement processes that require humans to match thousands of invoices to purchase orders. HR workflows that require people to manually enter data between systems. Customer service responses that follow scripts so rigid they might as well be automated. Each discovery opens new possibilities for exponential improvement.

3. Create Outcomes-Driven Metrics

Exponential thinking changes everything about how work is evaluated and rewarded. Traditional metrics count activities such as calls made, tickets closed, and reports filed. Exponential metrics measure outcomes such as revenue per employee, problems solved per person, and cycle-time compression.

When we implemented this way of managing work at Automation Anywhere, we discovered 40% of customer service requests needed no human involvement at all. But this insight only emerged when we stopped measuring "tickets handled" and started measuring "problems solved autonomously." The metric shift revealed that many "customer service interactions" were just information retrieval that never required human involvement on our end.

The Brazilian energy company's transformation accelerated when it stopped measuring "tax processing per day" and started measuring "tax optimization per employee." The old metric encouraged hiring more people to process faster. The new metric encouraged people to find ways to create exponentially more value.

4. Think in Terms of Digital Workers

What if every person in your company had ten AI agents as direct reports? This reframing transforms AI from a threat to human employment into an amplifier of human capability. You're not replacing humans with machines – you're giving humans superhuman leverage.

Jane doesn't lose her job to AI. Jane becomes a team of eleven – herself plus ten digital workers handling everything that doesn't require human creativity, strategy, empathy, or judgment. She shifts from doing to directing, from executing tasks to designing solutions. She is the same person with exponentially more impact. This model makes the math of The Five-Year Century work in your favor. If every worker becomes 10× more productive through AI, the demographic cliff becomes an opportunity to reimagine work itself.

There is an uncomfortable truth we must continue to address regarding those who won't adapt to the new world. Not everyone will make the transition to use AI effectively in their work. Some people – and organizations as a whole – will find endless reasons why exponential change won't work. They'll demand proof that doesn't exist yet, guarantees that nobody can provide, and permission from superiors who don't understand the question. This will accelerate the gap that will likely widen with every quarter in which those who don't reskill themselves with AI will be far less productive than those who do.

But this shouldn't prevent leaders from aiming for 10× thinking from their teams. Some colleagues may just be anxious about what's ahead. They may have built expertise in roles, systems, and processes that they fear may become obsolete. They may have invested years in skills that AI can replicate in seconds. Fear is rational when your professional identity is threatened. Leaders who acknowledge this anxiety among their teams while showing a path forward will find most people capable of remarkable reinvention when given tools, training, encouragement, and time to learn.

The best leaders will always encourage their teams and show them the possibilities of an exponential future.

5

The Illusion of Human-Only Work

Why We Confuse Machine Capabilities with Human Strength

What makes you irreplaceable at work?

Most business leaders reach for the same answers – judgment, context, pattern recognition, reading between the lines, sensing when something "doesn't add up." These are the competencies we were taught define professional strength.

But modern executives must confront a harder question: *What if these aren't the sources of your exceptional value at all?*

A chief technology officer we worked with spent nearly three decades at one of America's largest and most prestigious daily newspapers watching the media industry wrestle with this. As CTO, he'd seen every technological wave hit media – from monopoly to near-collapse. When he joined, newspapers controlled distribution, pricing, and audience access. They decided what people read, when they read it, and how much they paid. Scarcity powered everything – circulation, advertising, and influence.

Then the internet erased scarcity almost overnight. Print advertising migrated to Google and Facebook. Classifieds vanished into Craigslist. News became infinite, instantaneous, and largely free of charge. Social media replaced front pages as the primary gateway to information. For two decades, most publishers fought a slow retreat – cutting staff, shrinking pages, consolidating ownership, and trying to extract profit from a transformed model.

With the rise of LLMs and as agentic AI further matured, the CTO's team – along with some nudging from the newspaper's owners – decided to think differently. Instead of continuing to play defense to protect the "special" parts of their work, they asked a more fundamental question: *Which parts of the media business model were actually robotic – and why were humans still doing them?*

They didn't start with newsrooms. They started with invoices.

■ ■ ■

The news organization faced a familiar enterprise finance problem. Invoices came in wildly different formats. Tax structures varied by jurisdiction. The volume was overwhelming. The team couldn't verify every item, so overpayments and errors slipped through.

Most organizations would hire more staff or accept the losses. The CTO's team instead applied a simple rule: if the work requires perfect consistency at scale, it's machine work – no matter how sophisticated it once appeared.

This challenged more than a business model. It challenged a century of management doctrine.

Consider what contract review or tax compliance requires: judgment, regulatory knowledge, attention to detail, pattern recognition, and contextual reasoning. These are the very skills we've long considered uniquely human – and precisely what AI now performs better, faster, and cheaper.

This confusion is older than AI. The Industrial Age taught us to celebrate human consistency, speed, accuracy, and rule-following – capabilities only valued because machines couldn't yet deliver them. For decades we judged human exceptionalism by machine metrics: speed, consistency, error-free repetition, and pattern recognition at scale. We trained professionals to excel at tasks that were – at their core – machine-suited. Creative industries, finance, and legal teams all built careers on structured, pattern-based work that AI now handles effortlessly.

The Industrial Age told us humans were exceptional because they could perform repetitive work with precision. AI reveals that this was never the source of human value.

The real question is: What happens when machines finally take over machine work, and we can see human work for what it truly is?

How We Learned to Value the Wrong Work

Mirroring the CTO's perspectives, an IT and engineering leader working on his team saw the media's evolution up close. He remembers when journalistic excellence was defined, rightly, by judgment, creativity, and trusted human sources – capabilities no machine could replicate. However, the work of producing journalism also included vast amounts of mechanical labor: filing-cabinet factchecking, deadline-driven production workflows, advertising placement, pagination, and manual page layout.[1] These were not expressions of human insight; they were machine tasks carried out by people because no alternative yet existed.

Those were also the parts of the job few entered journalism to do. Today, newsrooms are able to embrace AI and automation to absorb this operational burden – automating transcription, tagging, archival search, layout, and production logistics – so human reporters and editors can concentrate on investigation, narrative, and accountability. The goal is not to replace journalism, but to restore it to its highest human form.

While it may have shifted the economics, the internet should have never truly threatened journalism itself. It disrupted the *machine work* journalists had been forced to perform alongside their human work. In some ways, the industry failed to distinguish between the two. It misunderstood what makes human contribution in journalism genuinely irreplaceable.

■ ■ ■

May 11, 1997, should have taught us everything we needed to know about this confusion. World chess champion Garry Kasparov slumped in his chair, defeated by IBM's Deep Blue. The match itself was a spectacle. Over 200 reporters descended on New York, millions watched worldwide, and IBM's stock price rose $3.6 billion during the event.[2] The final score was 3.5 to 2.5. It couldn't have been closer.[3]

Kasparov himself initially wrote that Deep Blue was "Intelligent the way your programmable alarm clock is intelligent. Not that losing to a $10 million alarm clock made me feel any better."[4] But after his first match with Deep Blue in 1996, which he won 4-2, he said, "I could feel. I could smell a new kind of intelligence across the table."[5]

What Kasparov sensed was something we're only now beginning to understand. Chess is designed for finding the shortest path to a goal through calculation and pattern recognition at a scale humans can't sustain compared to machines. We just didn't have machines capable of defeating us in it until that moment.

Fast forward to March 2016, and we repeated the pattern. Google's AlphaGo faced World Champion Lee Sedol. For those unfamiliar with Go, imagine chess but exponentially more complex. Played on a 19 × 19 grid with black and white stones, the objective is to surround more territory than your opponent. While chess has about 10^{120} possible games, Go has 10^{360}, more than the number of atoms in the observable universe.

On Move 37, AlphaGo made a play no human would consider. Commentators initially called it an error. Then they recognized its brilliance.[6] The match captivated 200 million viewers globally, with 60 million watching in China alone.[7] After that move, Sedol left the room for 15 minutes. "I was in shock. I was powerless," he later said.[8]

By 2019, Lee Sedol retired from professional Go entirely, citing machine dominance. "Even if I become number one, there is an entity that cannot be defeated."[9] The game's greatest modern champion simply gave up.

Then came 2022. DALL-E and ChatGPT arrived. Suddenly, AI could create stunning original artwork.[10] It could write poetry that makes your breakup texts look amateur. It could generate images indistinguishable from human-created work.

By 2024, Claude wrote code autonomously, achieving 71.7% on SWE-bench, up from 4.4% just one year earlier.[11] Performance differences between AI models dropped from 11.9 to 5.4% in one year.[12]

Cost reduction? A 280-fold decrease for GPT-3.5 level performance.[13] Advanced AI is now becoming a commodity, not a luxury. And in 2026, a number of engineers and technology leaders are hinting at artificial general intelligence (AGI) being just around the corner, although this is debatable depending on who you talk to.

Each time AI masters something we thought required human intelligence, we discover we were measuring human value by machine standards all along.

■ ■ ■

The leading American newspaper we've been discussing had to evaluate dozens of AI companies making bold claims. But the CTO and his team weren't just looking for more automation – they already had 30 automations running deterministic tasks and all of their infrastructure in the cloud. What they needed wasn't incremental efficiency. They needed AI and process models that could handle variability, understand context, and make intelligent decisions for business-critical processes that cut across departments.

Like others on the journey towards bold transformation, the news organization's leadership had to break through several psychological barriers that Harvard Business School researchers have identified that can turn highly capable executives into defenders of machine work.[14] These aren't doubts about AI. They're about identity: our sense of value tied to performing machine work well.

Once you understand these biases as barriers to success, you start noticing them everywhere.

Opacity Bias comes first: *"I don't understand it, so I can't trust it."* The black-box objection persists even though most humans can't explain how they do their jobs either. Ask an author how they wrote their book and you'll hear vague inspiration. Ask AI how it produced a response and it will usually walk you through the steps. Opacity Bias keeps us doing machine work we don't understand – just because we're more comfortable when *we* are the black box.

Emotionlessness Bias says: *"It can't feel, so it can't understand."* We assume tasks like customer service require emotion, though data repeatedly shows AI outperforming humans at understanding requests, anticipating outcomes, and detecting anomalies. Often the "human judgment" we claim to need is really just a misplaced understanding of human value.

Rigidity Bias is the belief that *"AI can't handle unique situations."* This "uniqueness neglect" convinces leaders that their business is too special for AI – even when they use the same accounting, supply chain, or compliance frameworks as everyone else. AI handles edge cases better because it draws from millions of examples. Rigidity Bias protects our supposed monopoly on pattern recognition – a monopoly we never actually had.

The Autonomy Threat exposes the deepest fear: *"I need to stay in control."* This bias literally costs lives. 76% of people feel unsafe in autonomous vehicles despite strong safety data.[15] As Neil deGrasse Tyson notes, America tolerates 35,000 road deaths a year but panics at the idea of 6,000 software-related fatalities – even if 29,000 people survive who would otherwise have died. We're bad drivers afraid of good drivers.[16]

These biases don't just shape individuals – they can shape entire organizations and industries. The 2023 Writers' Strike is often mischaracterized as a blanket rejection of AI, but that wasn't what actually happened. At its core, the strike was about power, pay, and authorship in a streaming-era economy where residuals had collapsed and studios were seeking to redefine creative labor. AI became a flashpoint not because writers directly opposed AI tools, but because they feared losing credit, compensation, and control if AI-generated material were used to devalue human authorship. Many writers were already experimenting with AI as a productivity aid and just didn't want it to be seen as a replacement for them entirely. The conflict wasn't human creativity versus machines; it was human creators versus systems that sought to extract more output while paying less for it.

The CTO's team within the news organization also encountered these biases everywhere. Finance staff feared their expertise would lose value. Legal teams argued that contract review required irreplaceable human judgment. Reporters worried about AI replacing journalists. Editors insisted AI couldn't grasp context.

They were partly right. Some tasks in their job descriptions would become less valuable. AI can replicate the machine-work parts of their roles. But they were asking the wrong question: Not "Can AI do my job?" but "Which parts of my job are machine work that keep me from the human work?"

What Makes Humans Truly Exceptional (And Why It Finally Matters)

This raises the boardroom-level question: *What remains uniquely human when AI handles so much of the work we've grown accustomed to?*

Start with consciousness. The Industrial Age taught us consciousness didn't matter – follow the process, be consistent, and execute. But consciousness is how leaders set vision and decide which goals matter. It's how organizations create meaning beyond transactions. Shareholders want returns, but they also want coherence. That requires someone asking, "Why are we doing this?" not just "How do we do this faster?"

Next is genuine empathy. AI can simulate empathetic responses with flawless consistency, but simulation isn't empathy. Real empathy is breaking rules for human reasons: waiving a late fee because someone's life is unraveling, asking why turnover is rising, and not just how to reduce it. Human empathy creates culture and loyalty – two things machines can't produce.

Then comes moral reasoning. Humans are inconsistent, contradictory, and situational. AI may be ethically consistent, but consistency isn't morality. Morality means weighing competing values and taking responsibility for the tradeoffs. It's the hiring manager who rejects the perfect resume because "something feels off," or the executive who forgoes profit because the human cost is too high.

And finally, creativity. Most "creative" work during the Industrial Age wasn't Michelangelo – it was today's equivalent of banner ads, social copy, and logo iterations. AI can handle that production work easily now. A real example of creativity from a business perspective is the work the news organization is doing inside its enterprise: reimagining the media business model for an AI world, reinventing identity, building trust with readers, and deciding which stories matter. That's human creativity.

The news organization stopped defending what made them "special" and started exploring what made them capable. Organizations that defend yesterday's uniqueness stagnate; those that explore tomorrow's capabilities transform.

But the more interesting question is: *What are humans doing with the time AI frees?*

■ ■ ■

We don't have data for every role, but we do know what happens when machine work disappears. At the Mayo Clinic, over 200 AI projects run through a clinician-led enablement team. Doctors design their own tools – so they design for the work doctors *should* do, not the machine tasks they were forced to do.[17]

FDA-cleared algorithms now detect heart disease with accuracy beyond human capability. In Mayo's EAGLE study, AI flagged five new cases of low ejection fraction per 1,000 patients – silent heart failures doctors routinely miss.[18] That's pattern recognition at scale, done perfectly, without fatigue.

John Halamka, Mayo Clinic Platform president, is blunt: "If your doctor could be replaced by AI, your doctor should be replaced by AI. . . Doctors and nurses who use AI will replace doctors and nurses who don't."[19]

Doctors who embrace AI spend less time scanning images and more time explaining what patterns mean. Less time documenting, more time thinking. They build trust, comfort scared patients, deliver difficult news with empathy, and celebrate improvements with joy. That is what makes doctors – and all of us – truly exceptional; not our pattern recognition, but our humanity.

In large healthcare systems, AI-driven scheduling, documentation, and intake automation have returned hours per week to clinicians – time now reinvested in patient care instead of administrative backlogs.

In finance, Goldman Sachs deployed AI assistants to roughly 10,000 employees, with a broader rollout underway.[20] Engineers are already seeing 20% efficiency gains – astonishing given the company's already high productivity bar. Junior bankers who once spent

100-hour weeks formatting reports now compress days of work into hours.

Goldman Sachs CEO David Solomon revealed a more radical shift: AI can draft 95% of an IPO prospectus in minutes.[21] Work that required six-person teams grinding for weeks – analyzing financials, crafting narratives, ensuring compliance – now happens as fast as ordering DoorDash.

The impact isn't just efficiency. Bankers freed from formatting PowerPoints and drafting boilerplate prospectuses now focus on strategy, client relationships, and opportunity recognition. They negotiate complex deals, mentor junior staff, and help shape the culture that makes their organization distinctive.

Elsewhere, at leading global consultancies, automation has eliminated thousands of hours of manual audit sampling and reconciliation, allowing professionals to concentrate on interpretation, anomalies, and client insight rather than spreadsheet mechanics.

Factory floors in Munich and Toyota City show the same pattern. BMW's collaborative AI systems improve quality control and reduce errors in real time – adaptive systems that learn from human expertise rather than simply following scripts.

Toyota went further, enabling factory workers to build machine learning models without writing code.[22] Workers with decades of domain knowledge created more than 10,000 models, saving over 10,000 labor hours.[23] They encoded expertise about bottlenecks, late suppliers, and subtle machine failures into systems that scale across the entire operation. Supply chain efficiency improved 35%.

But the deeper shift is philosophical. Toyota proved AI augmentation isn't limited to knowledge workers. The person installing windshields for 20 years knows more about windshields than any engineer. Give that person AI tools, and expertise scales beyond their individual hands.

These workers now design AI systems, consult on process improvements, and focus on meaningful bottlenecks while machines handle the routine. Blue-collar workers are building AI models more effectively than MIT grads who've never held a torque wrench – because judgment about what matters remains human.

Neuroscience helps explain why this partnership works. Your brain runs out of steam halfway through the day. Humans make over 10,000 decisions daily, once you cross that threshold – typically mid-afternoon – your cognitive performance drops. You absorb less information. A 50-page report becomes hieroglyphics. Complex analysis is replaced by gut instinct.

AI's value isn't speed alone – it's cognitive preservation. By taking thousands of micro-decisions off your plate, AI protects your limited mental battery so you can focus on high-stakes decisions. Your brain is a Fortune 500 CEO forced to sort mail. AI becomes your cognitive bodyguard, absorbing the mental hits so your best thinking survives.

Humans excel at edge cases – situations no manual anticipates. We negotiate exceptions, interpret motivations, build trust, and set vision. AI excels at pattern recognition, consistency, and scale. It never tires, forgets, or loses focus after lunch.

Together, humans and AI create what MIT calls "Complementary Team Performance."[24] It's not one plus one equals two – it's one plus one equals eleven. Humans bring context; AI brings scale. Together, they're unstoppable.

Garry Kasparov proved this with advanced chess. Human-AI teams consistently beat grandmasters and supercomputers. Humans provide strategy and psychology; AI provides calculation and pattern recognition. Kasparov later noted that AI helped him ask better questions and explore strategies no human would consider. AI made him more human by freeing him to do the human work of chess – vision, strategy, and creativity.

Ultimately, the real human role isn't solving problems – it's deciding which problems matter. AI will only do what humans direct it to do. We steer the power.

■　■　■

The news organization's transformation shows what it looks like to abandon the illusion that human value depends on doing machine work. Their strategy – "AI everywhere" – means AI handles machine work everywhere so humans can do human work everywhere.[25]

Within a year, the news organization generated millions in automation value. They eliminated tax overpayments. Their AI agents now read, extract, and validate every invoice for tax accuracy. After finance validated the model, legal used it to redline contracts, rapidly expanding ROI across functions with minimal lift.

Once the proof of concept existed in the finance department, other departments also started asking, "What work can this technology take off my hands to free up more of my time?" Legal started using it to automatically redline contracts. The technology unlocked additional ROI with minimal implementation effort, positioning the company to further reduce manual workloads and scale valuable impact across multiple functions.[26]

The news organization's CFO shared a perspective on ROI that reveals how successful organizations think about transformation. He told the CTO something that drives finance teams crazy but captures the truth about technology adoption. "The exercise here isn't to justify that when we spend this much on automation, we get this much return. That's not the right way to look at it." There's a leap of faith element, he explained, similar to when organizations debated moving to the cloud. You could spend five years analyzing spreadsheets comparing capital investments in data centers versus cloud costs, and all you'd accomplish is putting yourself five years behind where everyone else is.[27]

The news organization expects to do far more than break-even on its AI investment, and IT leadership is equally clear about the learning curve component. "We're investing in climbing the adoption curve. In years two, three, and four, we can't fully imagine all the things we're going to be able to do with this technology."[28]

This is exponential thinking. Don't protect yesterday's advantages; create tomorrow's outcomes.

The CTO's leadership reflects this thinking. "We're not moving slowly," he said. "We're moving with speed and scale. This technology is real and there's only one conclusion. Move fast, scale fast, don't blink."[29]

What are the humans at the prestigious news organization doing with their new free time? Their go-forward strategy provides the answer. As a tech and media company with an established in-house ML, Data, and AI Analytics team, they're investing in packaging their proprietary LLMs to enhance customer and reader experience in innovative ways, and to generate new revenue streams by syndicating their LLM agents' knowledge base to other major LLMs.[30]

Put in other words, they're not just using AI, they're creating AI products. They're monetizing their AI expertise. They're turning the technology that automates their operations into a revenue stream. That's strategy. That's vision. That's opportunity recognition. That's humans doing human work, choosing the path and letting AI identify the shortest routes at each turn.

And they're asking questions machines can't: What do readers need? What is journalism when information is abundant? How do we create value when content is free?

■ ■ ■

At Automation Anywhere, we've automated 46% of our HR operations – the equivalent of 12 full-time employees – and expect to reach 70% in 2026, with zero job losses. Humans are redirected to strategic work. Employees using AI agents report higher satisfaction; those least comfortable with AI report the lowest. Manager scores improve immediately.

The pattern is clear: people using AI are happier. They're freed from machine work and finally using the judgment, creativity, and strategic thinking that drew them to the job. Gen Z will arrive with AI and automation experience already; they won't tolerate work that machines can do.

The new human role is orchestrator of intelligence. You set vision, relationships, and meaning. AI does the mechanical work. Machines help as playmakers; humans become the quarterback.

A conversation with a senior IT service-desk manager captured the shift more clearly than any abstract theory. For years, his team had been buried under password resets, ticket triage, and routine incidents – hundreds per day. After deploying AI agents, up to 80% of those requests were resolved automatically. At first, the team worried about relevance. Six months later, they were running proactive security analyses, redesigning employee experience workflows, and meeting directly with business leaders to prevent problems before they surfaced. Their jobs didn't disappear. Their impact exploded.

What changed wasn't the number of people. It was the altitude of their work.

For leaders, the essential question becomes: What would you do if you had ten AI agents as direct reports? You'll discover extraordinary talent that was previously trapped inside low-value tasks.

And when an employee worries that AI will take their job, walk them through the task map. Show them which activities are machine work, and which are human work. Excel didn't eliminate accountants; it eliminated the math that kept them from being advisors. Every role has this same dividing line. Your obligation as a leader is to help people cross it.

This is the choice in front of every organization: defend yesterday's machine work or invest in tomorrow's human work. The leaders who move fastest – like Kasparov in chess or the news organization we've been discussing – don't ask whether AI threatens them. They ask how to use it to amplify what humans do best.

AI-first transformation starts with one set of practical steps: audit the work, separate human tasks from machine tasks, and think about where to deploy AI to remove repetitive processes across the company. Then, give people the time and tools to do the work only humans can do. *Finally.*

■   ■   ■

The Leader's Playbook: Delivering Meaningful Human Impact

Senior leaders have the ability to turn AI into a human-impact engine – not an IT project. This is not a technology rollout. It is a redefinition of how work is divided between humans and machines. Leaders who treat it as software adoption will underperform. Leaders who treat it as an operating model redesign will compound advantage.

1. Start with an "Enterprise Hot Spot Analysis" – Not an AI Strategy

Before selecting tools, platforms, or vendors, leaders must first surface where enterprise value is leaking because humans are doing machine work. The enterprise hot spot analysis is not an inventory exercise; it is a broader business value assessment. The goal is to identify high-friction work across departments where automation and AI can unlock immediate capacity, cash flow, margin, speed, or customer impact, such as within finance, supply chain, manufacturing, IT, customer service, sales operations, and HR.

In each function, you can identify a large amount of cost savings and efficiency gains by focusing on any processes that exhibit at least one of the following signals:

- High manual-touch volume or handoffs
- Deterministic inputs and repeatable outputs
- Rule-based decisions or threshold approvals
- Work created primarily for reporting, reconciliation, compliance, or formatting
- Bottlenecks that delay revenue, hiring, fulfillment, or customer resolution

At the board level, the framing into a business value assessment shifts from software ROI to operating leverage: *What percentage of total enterprise labor hours are currently consumed by deterministic, machine-executable work? What would it mean for growth, resilience, and talent if even 20–30% of that capacity were redeployed?*

2. Make the "Ten AI Direct Reports" a Formal Leadership Exercise

Every senior leader must be able to answer, "If you had ten AI agents reporting to you tomorrow, what would you have them do, and what would you do with your extra free time?"

Require them to complete a one-pager that redesigns how they would achieve their annual operating plan with this in mind. This can include identification of how they would redeploy human judgment, any new strategic capacity that could be created, and condensed timelines to deliver on priorities.

This exercise forces leaders to consider how much of their personal authority is tied to supervising AI-capable work instead of shaping critical business outcomes.

3. Reassign Ownership: Machines Own the Flowchart, Humans Own the Judgment

Formally rewrite role charters using a simple rule: If the task can be diagrammed as a flowchart, it is no longer a human responsibility.

For every role, you can create a two-column job design:

- **Machine-Owned Work:** Includes items such as intake triage, first-draft generation, extraction, validation, reconciliation, reporting, documentation and scheduling
- **Human-Owned Work:** Includes items such as strategic decision-making, exception handling, relationship management, moral judgment, innovation and problem selection

4. Deploy AI in 90-Day Revenue, Cost, or Capacity Sprints

Every sprint must be tied to one business P&L outcome, not "automation for automation's sake." Each sprint should target a bottleneck that constrains an outcome like revenue growth, customer experience, cycle time, cost or working capital. The outcomes allow you to measure results in dollars, days, decisions accelerated or customers retained. The goal is to eliminate at least 20% of the manual handling of that process. Any AI deployment that does not show measurable business impact in 90 days is paused or killed. This sustains executive credibility and prevents "AI theater."

5. Redesign Incentives So Humans Don't Defend Machine Work

Every defensive behavior described in this chapter is reinforced by incentive design. To truly accelerate the throttle, leaders should consider a recalibration of bonus structures tied to volume, throughput, utilization or manual tasks output. In exchange, you want to reward around metrics for cross-functional problem-solving, automation adoption and other high-value outcomes.

Example Metrics:

Traditional Metrics:	AI-First Metrics:
Tickets closed	Percentage of tickets fully automated
Reports produced	Decisions accelerated by AI
Hours worked	Cycle time eliminated
Team size	Revenue/cost per human

Most companies say, "use AI," but *no one gets paid for actually doing it*. You can fix that.

You can consider tying a meaningful portion of variable compensation to AI integration. This is where an employee could say "20% of my annual bonus is based on how effectively I use AI to remove manual work from my role and my team's workflows." Key components could include AI utilization rate, percent of role tasks automated, new workflows generated using AI agents, verified cycle-time reduction, and more.

As importantly, team bonuses can be connected to outcomes achieved plus automation integrated. In this way, a team that hits revenue targets *with high automation* out-earns a team that hits numbers using brute human force.

Lastly, it's critical for AI-first enterprises to have executive bonus design built around AI adoption. This is where a significant portion of compensation is paid based on the ability to deliver the new AI-first operating model, with KPIs such as speed-to-value from AI investments, adoption rates, percentage of core processes done with AI agents, and more. This is critical to prevent AI theater at the top and reinforce the need for leadership to play an active role in delivery of accelerated outcomes.

AI-first organizations aren't built by adopting more technology, but by leaders who redesign work, incentives, and accountability so machines do machine work, and humans are paid to do what only humans can do.

6

The Illusion of Hierarchical Control

The Breakdown Between Knowing and Doing

What happens when the people doing the work know exactly how to fix it – but nobody will listen?

An executive director leading agentic and automation transformation at one of the Big Four professional services firms watched his teams confront this frustration daily. Across the organization, frontline workers identified inefficiencies everywhere. Audit teams manually reconciled thousands of transactions. HR staff scheduled interviews by hand, tracking candidates through endless email threads. Finance professionals chased receipts one at a time, verifying tax amounts on invoices formatted differently by hundreds of vendors. The problems were obvious. The solutions were clear. Yet nothing changed.

Awareness was never the issue. The professional services firm had identified $150 million in automation opportunities scattered across the enterprise. The people closest to the work already knew where every dollar was hiding. They understood which processes wasted the most time, which systems generated chronic bottlenecks, and which workflows trapped talented people in repetitive, low-value tasks. This knowledge didn't live in strategy documents or consultant slide decks.

It lived inside the daily experience of 275,000 employees across 142 countries who understood precisely what needed to be fixed.[1]

The barrier was the chasm between knowing and doing. Even simple automation required navigating a gauntlet of approvals, each adding weeks or months. By the time an idea reached someone with budget authority, the person who spotted it had moved on to the next fire drill. Momentum evaporated in committee meetings. Innovation drowned in approval chains.

Hierarchy wasn't enabling change. It was suffocating it.

The executive director saw the problem clearly and made a decision that inverted traditional change management. Instead of issuing directives or hiring consultants to chart transformation pathways, he recognized where true expertise resided. "We have tons of AI agents and skills available, but the process is yours," he told teams. "You decide what skills to use and where."[2]

The professional services firm began empowering the people who actually do the work to lead the change. The central team provided the software platform and a governance framework, but the rest was up to individual teams. HR teams surfaced their own automation opportunities. Finance built its own solutions. Audit defined its own priorities. The hierarchy wasn't orchestrating the transformation. It was providing a framework and stepping aside.

We must shatter the illusion that wisdom flows downward from executive offices or that transformation succeeds because senior leaders decree it. It is irrational to believe that people who haven't done frontline work in years somehow know best how to improve it. In the industrial age, when work was predictable and change happened slowly, hierarchical control made sense. Today, when insight can become obsolete within months, hierarchy doesn't just slow progress – it can destroy it.

Here's a question that might make some executives uneasy: when was the last time you actually performed the work your organization sells? Not managed it, strategized about it, or presented it – but performed it, installed the product, processed the transaction, served the customer, and wrote the code. For most senior leaders, the answer is measured in years, not months. Yet these same leaders decide how that work should change.

Transformation statistics tell a harsh story. According to McKinsey, roughly 70% of major change initiatives fail.[3] This means that a broad majority of organizations that invest heavily in transformation end up falling short. In one global survey, McKinsey found that of the transformations rated "not at all successful," 70% had been planned by ten or fewer people – a tiny circle of leaders designing change for everyone else. In another, when transformations failed to engage line managers and frontline employees, only about 3% were judged successful; when those groups were involved, reported success rates rose to around a quarter.[4]

Hierarchy creates what can only be described as reality distortion fields. Each management layer adds its own narrative, filters out bad news, and packages information into slide-deck-ready abstractions. Customer complaints become "service delivery opportunities." Technical debt becomes "legacy system optimization." Competitive threats become "market dynamics we're monitoring." By the time insights reach decision-makers, they no longer reflect the truth on the ground.

The professional services firm experienced this directly. Its HR department was overwhelmed by manual interview scheduling, juggling hundreds of candidates across emails, calendars, and spreadsheets. Delays frustrated applicants and hiring managers alike, damaging the employer brand while consuming enormous amounts of staff time.

A traditional response would have been to commission studies, form steering committees, or hire consultants to map the hiring journey. Instead, the professional services firm worked with Automation Anywhere and took a simpler approach: they asked the HR team what they needed and gave them the tools to build it. The team automated interview scheduling, eliminating a coordination nightmare that had persisted for years. The solution wasn't complex. It simply worked.

Frontline experts had always understood the issue better than the C-suite ever could. They knew which emails routinely went missing, which calendar conflicts were most damaging, and which manual steps exhausted the team. They didn't need permission to diagnose the problem. They needed permission to solve it.

As executives debate AI governance, convene committees, and draft policies, 93% of Gen Z workers already use two or more AI tools weekly – many without IT approval. This isn't recklessness; it's a signal. The workforce is moving faster than the control structures designed to manage it. Governance and security are absolutely critical in an AI-first world – but when they become gatekeeping functions rather than enabling frameworks, they push innovation into the shadows instead of shaping it in the open. The risk isn't that employees move too fast. The risk is that leadership moves too slowly to guide them.

The speed gap is staggering. A junior developer armed with tools like Cursor or Claude can now outperform entire experienced teams trapped in legacy processes.

Startups make decisions in days while corporations take months. Academic research shows each management layer adds about 2.5 days to decision cycles. In The Five-Year Century, those 2.5 days could translate into meaningful competitive disadvantage.

Leadership within the professional services firm recognized this urgency. After HR's success, they didn't stop. They expanded automation into finance and accounting, then across other domains. Each win helped build momentum for the next. The instinct of hierarchy would have been to centralize, standardize, create templates, and impose paralyzing governance from above. But instead, they took the opposite path. They gave teams autonomy to identify opportunities and build solutions using Automation Anywhere's platform. The result: over 150 automations delivering $90 million in measurable value.

Transformation didn't emerge from an executive strategy or a consultant's roadmap. It emerged from trusting 275,000 employees who understood their work better than any centralized team ever could. The hierarchy didn't drive change. It enabled change by guiding it and then getting out of the way.

The Democratic Revolution in Decision-Making

To understand why hierarchical control persists despite its failures, we need to return to 1945. World War II had just ended, and American business leaders looked to the military for organizational inspiration. The War Production Board had coordinated production on a staggering scale. Military command structures mobilized millions and defeated fascism. Surely such systems could run factories and insurance companies.

And, for a time, they could. The military model worked brilliantly for predictable, repetitive tasks performed in stable markets with capital intensity and slow-moving competition. Alfred Sloan used divisional hierarchy to build General Motors into one of the world's dominant industrial enterprises. IBM's carefully engineered bureaucracy – "Big Blue" – became the gold standard of corporate order in the early information age. Decisions flowed downward. Inefficient, yes – but effective in an era of slow change and limited competition.

Then the world shifted. The Information Age arrived, but our organizational structures didn't evolve. Instead, we doubled down. We industrialized management. We created entire certification ecosystems around bureaucratic oversight. The Project Management Institute turned work organization into a ritual of process, documentation, and compliance – an industry built on managing complexity that often exists because the managers themselves created it.

Most organizational charts resemble archaeological digs – layers of leadership accumulated over decades. Each layer adds a gatekeeper, an approval step, another meeting. When customer feedback or frontline insight emerges, it must climb the entire ladder. Each level asks, "Did you follow the process?" By the time information reaches decision-makers, the market has already moved.

Hierarchy grounds both engines of the modern enterprise, and it does so in different but equally damaging ways. The productivity engine slows as every additional layer inserts friction: approvals replace action, coordination replaces execution, and decision latency compounds until speed itself becomes a competitive liability. At the same time, an already slimming workforce gets further reduced in output when capable people spend their days seeking permission instead of solving problems or navigating org charts instead of creating value.

The professional services firm we've been referencing could have fallen into the hierarchy trap. With 150+ automations deployed, the instinct would have been to centralize control and tighten governance. Instead, they moved from traditional Robotic Process Automation (RPA) towards Agentic Process Automation (APA) – combining document automation with AI agents capable of understanding internal knowledge and generating new learning autonomously. This evolution wasn't dictated from above. It emerged from teams pushing boundaries on their own.

■ ■ ■

The AI-driven intelligence revolution has broken every assumption that once justified hierarchy. A first-year employee who uses TikTok may understand modern consumer engagement better than a CMO with decades of TV advertising experience. A 23-year-old developer in Bangalore may generate product ideas that outperform a seasoned director's entire roadmap.

What happens when frontline workers can tap into analytical tools that once belonged only to strategy teams, see cross-enterprise data that used to be reserved for the C-suite, and move with the execution speed of a startup founder?

This is no longer theoretical. It is an emerging reality.

AI doesn't merely automate tasks. It democratizes capability. A retail associate can run demand forecasts once reserved for teams of analysts. A bank teller can make better lending recommendations with AI-driven decision support instead of waiting on a manager. A junior engineer using AI coding copilots and agents can rival the output of entire senior teams. At JPMorgan, for example, an AI system reviewing commercial loan contracts now saves about 360,000 work hours a year – roughly 170–180 full-time roles worth of time – while the bank's generative AI assistant is being rolled out to about 140,000 employees to boost productivity across the enterprise.[5]

Generational dynamics intensify this shift. While many senior leaders may be early in their journey to understand LLMs and attend their first AI workshops, younger employees are already quietly building workflows and solving problems with tools they discovered on their own. That doesn't make late adopters obsolete, however. The competitive risk isn't admitting, "I'm still learning this." The risk is treating AI as optional. In a few years, saying you don't "need" AI will sound a lot like saying you don't need electricity: technically possible, but strategically ungrounded.

Gartner predicts that in 2026, 20% of organizations will eliminate half of middle-management roles.[6] This isn't a reduction of people displaced by AI – it's a reduction of roles that consume human potential through bureaucratic coordination. The individuals in these jobs aren't the problem. The roles themselves are artifacts of a pre-AI era.

The Market Rewards Less Hierarchy

The leadership transformation required here challenges everything taught in business school. As a leader, you are no longer a general commanding troops. You're more like a conductor of an orchestra that can play the notes without you. Your value isn't in telling musicians which notes to play but in creating conditions where beautiful music emerges naturally.

Take Amazon's two-pizza teams principle: any team should be small enough to be fed with two pizzas.[7] This isn't about catering budgets. It's about creating units small enough that everyone knows each other's strengths, nimble enough to pivot without dozens of approval meetings, and powerful enough to change how the company operates. These teams have autonomous decision-making within defined parameters. The conductor doesn't micromanage. They set the tempo and key, then let the musicians improvise.

Satya Nadella's transformation of Microsoft provides a masterclass in this new leadership. When he became CEO in 2014, Microsoft's market cap was around $300 billion. The company was stuck in internal warfare, with divisions competing against each other and a toxic forced-ranking system that made employees spend more time politicking than producing.[8]

What did Nadella do? He listened. Not performative town halls, but real conversations where he took notes and asked follow-up questions. Employees explained that forced ranking destroyed collaboration because helping a colleague might lower your own ranking. They showed him how Microsoft's obsession with Windows was preventing cloud growth. They identified the cultural challenges eating the company from within.

Nadella implemented their suggestions quickly. The result? Microsoft's market cap grew from $300 billion to over $3 trillion.[9] The transformation wasn't about strategy decks or reorganization charts. It was about humility. Nadella put it simply: "The C in CEO stands for curator of culture."

Best Buy's turnaround in the 2010s followed the same pattern. When former CEO Hubert Joly took over in 2012, the company was hemorrhaging money and being called "Amazon's showroom." His first move? He spent a week working in stores, wearing the blue shirt, listening to frontline workers.[10]

Employees told him the website search was broken, something headquarters missed because executives don't shop their own stores. They explained that the employee discount was worse than regular sale prices, making staff feel undervalued. They showed him how vendor-funded positions created conflicts of interest that undermined customer service. Joly listened to their suggestions and implemented them, and Best Buy went from billion-dollar losses to billion-dollar profits.

This is servant leadership in action. Your job isn't commanding compliance but enabling success. You remove obstacles rather than create approval processes. You amplify employee voices instead of filtering them into your "experience." Success isn't measured by how well people follow your orders but by how effectively they deliver results despite your presence.

The humility required here might feel like weakness to command-and-control types: Admitting you don't have all the answers; seeking input from younger, more technically skilled employees; and learning from failures instead of defending decisions. But in complex, rapidly changing environments, nobody has all the answers and that's okay.

AT&T's Project Raindrops further illustrates the power of distributed decision-making in flattened structures. Employees were allowed to eliminate outdated processes without approval when changes met simple criteria. Thousands of micro-improvements compounded into more than $230 million in savings. Small changes, multiplied across thousands of people, generated massive transformation.[11]

█ ▓ ▒

Hierarchy isn't simply being reformed in The Five-Year Century. It's being replaced by networks of human-AI collaboration where decisions occur wherever they are needed, with AI handling coordination traditionally performed by multiple management layers.

Automation Anywhere embraced this shift in our own support operations through Agentic Process Automation. By blending autonomous digital agents and human engineers in a flattened hierarchy, we achieved extraordinary results: 32% of support cases resolved autonomously, with resolution speeds 83% faster than traditional human-only workflows.

This approach turbocharges speed across industries. Banking AI enables instant decisions that once required days of analysis. Retail AI predicts demand in real time. Manufacturing AI optimizes production through thousands of micro-adjustments no human could track.

The professional services firm advanced even further by integrating Document Automation with AI agents designed to operate within a flattened decision structure, where knowledge and authority lived closest to the work. These agents didn't replace judgment or impose centralized rules. Instead, they absorbed institutional knowledge directly from frontline teams, interpreted context across documents and systems, and adapted as work changed. As teams used and refined them, the agents continuously improved, capturing patterns that would have been lost in traditional approval chains. The result was a shift from reactive problem-solving to proactive optimization, not because strategy changed at the top, but because learning accelerated at the edges of the organization.

Organizations thriving today aren't simply those with great strategies – they're the ones with antifragility built into their DNA. Distributed decision-making allows them to adapt under pressure rather than fracture.

Markets today often punish hierarchy and reward agility. Investors understand that hierarchical organizations may appear stable today but are structurally incapable of responding to tomorrow. Consider Tesla, where its market cap has been higher than GM, Ford, Toyota, and other car companies – combined.[12] Investors are not simply betting on who makes the best cars today. They're also betting on who can adapt fastest, deliver on innovation and meaningfully set up their company for future growth.

Customers expect rapid solutions, not explanations about internal approvals or processes. Talent markets favor organizations where employees have real autonomy. High performers don't want careers spent navigating bureaucracy – they want to build, solve, and see impact.

The people doing the work often already know what needs to change. Once you listen, you'll be astonished at what they build. And you'll see the market reward you, too.

■   ▨   ▩

The Leader's Playbook: Building Fast and Flat Teams

1. Flatten the Organization Around Outcomes, Not Functions

AI-first leaders should organize work around discrete, AI-enabled business outcomes rather than departmental silos. This means creating persistent, outcomes-driven teams where employees are accountable for achieving business results – not activities. The teams work with AI agents directly alongside them as digital workers. Teams are designed for fewer handoffs, more speed in delivery, and overall fewer managers managing people.

From an operations perspective, costs fall structurally, not through any one-time cuts, and revenue can accelerate as friction collapses. Flattened organizations have board-level KPIs such as revenue per employee, cost per transaction, and percentage of workflows running autonomously.

2. Move Authority to the Edge, Away from the Center

To break down hierarchy, you should transfer decision rights for automation and AI use cases to frontline teams with budget guardrails – not approval chains. This allows you to set financial and risk thresholds but remove any downstream approvals. It will give domain teams direct access to AI and automation platforms without undue constraints. Any steering committee oversight can be replaced with "build and measure" cycles that reinforce continuous improvement instead of hierarchical control.

The goal is to reinforce the cultural shift from permission-seeking to true change management ownership, where people are encouraged to operate with speed and an embrace for exponential thinking. Moving authority to the edges helps people see real business value that can be achieved instead of theoretical ROI.

3. Unleash Leaders as Curators of Culture – Not Controllers of Process

You should redefine executive responsibility from issuing directives to shaping trust, safety, innovation, and experimentation. What does this mean in practice? Publicly rewarding a growth mindset, learning from frontline feedback and acting on it, and embracing learnings from failures in a way that encourages rapid iteration. Leaders should elevate any employee-built AI solutions and automation processes, not just centrally-designed programs from corporate operations. This leads to faster adoption of AI across the enterprise and stronger retention of top talent.

4. Design for Continuous Compounding

Successful transformations should be designed as self-reinforcing systems, not programs with an end date. This requires treating automation as a permanent operating capability, funded like a growth engine rather than scoped as a one-time CapEx initiative aimed solely at linear cost reduction. As organizations mature, they can reinvest gains into deeper automation and intelligence, allowing each wave of success to fund the next. We have seen this repeatedly as customers extend proven RPA programs with AI-backed agentic capabilities, compounding value over time rather than resetting the business case with each new initiative.

Designing for continuous compounding gradually reshapes the organization's operating DNA. As automation handles predictable execution, human talent shifts from reactive problem-solving to proactive optimization – creating durable competitive advantage not through a single breakthrough, but through sustained, cumulative progress.

The future of work will be built by trusting the people closest to the work, giving them the tools to act, and designing systems that compound learning instead of slowing it down.

7

The Illusion of Technological Servitude

Why Are Humans Still Serving Technology?

Sarah's Tuesday began with the gentle chime of her smartphone alarm at 6:30 a.m., a soothing melody crafted by neuroscientists to ease people into wakefulness. By 8:45 a.m., she would be in her company's break room, professionally manicured nails digging crescents into her palms, locked in mortal combat with a coffee machine that insisted on a firmware update before it would dispense a single molecule of caffeine.

But we're getting ahead of ourselves.

The first warning sign arrived around 8:00 a.m., just as she settled into her ergonomically optimized workstation on the 37th floor of the Financial Tower. A small red banner blinked above her taskbar:

"Your password has expired. Click here to create a new one."

Sarah's stomach dropped. Had she been notified earlier that she needed to update her password?

The quarterly budget review started at 9:00 a.m. and she wanted to do final prep. She needed three documents from the Company Portal: last quarter's projections, the variance reports, and the updated forecast her team uploaded at 11:47 p.m. The previous night had been another "romantic evening with Excel," as her husband called it.

She clicked the banner. A cheerful dialog box bloomed across her screen:

Password requirements:

- Minimum 14 characters
- At least one uppercase letter
- At least one lowercase letter
- Two non-consecutive numbers
- One special character (!@#$%^&*)
- No username substrings
- Not one of your last 10 passwords
- Must not resemble passwords used on affiliated systems

Sarah stared at the list. Six years at the company meant she had already produced 24 increasingly desperate passwords. She had burned through the seasonal progression – 5thSpring2025!, 5thSummer2025!, 5thFall2025! – until IT's pattern-detection algorithm chastised her like a stern parent.

She finally succeeded in updating her password after entering the code received through push notifications on her smartphone – an achievement that felt less like progress and more like surviving a minor trial.

By the time she attempted to access the Company Portal again with her new password, the system was still having challenges recognizing her, so she had to restart her computer to get the issue resolved.

Sarah's psyche split. One part observed, almost academically, how a capable, highly educated professional had been reduced to digital servitude. The other part wanted to throw her laptop through the floor-to-ceiling windows that didn't open because the climate-control system knew better than she did what temperature she preferred.

She needed coffee.

The break room's new "smart coffee system" – installed as part of the company's "Digital Workplace of the Future" initiative – greeted her with a radiant touchscreen. She tapped "Cappuccino."

"PLEASE DOWNLOAD THE MORRISON CAFÉ EXPERI-
ENCE APP FOR FULL FUNCTIONALITY."

She downloaded the app. It required her to register as a user and do various authentications to connect her smartphone to the machine.

Sarah laughed. Softly at first, like someone reading a mildly amusing cartoon. Then harder. Within seconds, she stood alone in the break room, tears streaming, laughing at the absurdity of possessing advanced degrees, years of experience, and a high salary – yet lacking the ability to use her computer or get coffee.

"Everything okay, Sarah?" asked Marcus from Accounts Receivable. He held a chipped ceramic mug from ancient times, when humans just poured coffee from pots.

Sarah wiped her eyes. "Marcus, I've spent nearly an hour being rejected by four different systems that theoretically know who I am. And now –" she gestured at the coffee machine's screen, which had progressed to demanding a firmware update – "I'm denied caffeine by a device that needs new instructions on how to pour hot water over ground beans."

Marcus nodded sympathetically. "Yeah. . . the printer on 14 became self-aware and only prints in Wingdings." He shrugged. "Well, hope your day gets better, Sarah."

■ ■ ■

While perhaps a bit dramatized, Sarah's technology issues capture a snapshot of the reality for millions of knowledge workers. We've engineered a world where highly skilled professionals spend too much of their cognitive energy on password gymnastics, cumbersome UX navigation, and swivel chair work across an increasingly complex web of applications and system updates.

For example, the average knowledge worker toggles between nine applications just to complete daily tasks, loses 2.5 hours to inefficient systems, and pays a "cognitive switching tax" every time they move between tools.[1]

We take human minds built for creativity, strategy, problem-solving and complex reasoning and use them as sentient API connectors. It's like using a Ferrari to deliver newspapers.

Industrialization trained us to bend humans to machinery. Lucy Larcom from earlier in the story lived by the factory bell[2]:

4:30 a.m. – wake up.

5:00 a.m. – at the loom.

7:00 p.m. – collapse.

Machines received scheduled maintenance. Humans were expected to absorb the strain.

Lucy had factory bells. We have notifications and password resets – and no final bell to signal freedom.

During the ERP boom of the 1990s and 2000s, companies spent billions implementing monolithic systems with a success rate worse than a coin toss. Roughly 75% failed to meet objectives, with average costs around $9,000 per user, plus implementation expenses of up to 200% of the license fee. For a 1,000-employee company, that's $27 million invested in software that often failed to work as promised.[3]

We'd never accept a world where 75% of cars fail to start, phones fail to connect, or espresso machines fail to make our morning drink.

Yet we accept it in our digital infrastructure, often without question.

This quiet acceptance of broken systems creates a form of technological servitude, destroying value across all four responsibilities leaders are accountable for:

- **Revenue:** Highly trained employees lose 600+ hours per year fighting systems instead of creating, innovating, or serving customers.
- **Cost:** Inefficiencies compound well beyond cost of failed implementations as opportunity costs silently balloon.
- **Risk:** Cognitive overload leads to shortcuts and mistakes; surveys consistently show over 80% of tech workers reporting symptoms of near burnout.
- **Culture:** When tools are designed without regard for human limits, engagement erodes and even top talent disengages.

The damage accelerates in an always-on world. Average smartphone use has climbed from about 45 minutes per day in 2011 to more than five hours per day by 2025 – the equivalent of an additional 35 hours per week mediated through a glowing screen. For many employees, the workday no longer ends; it simply migrates from laptops to phones, from offices to bedrooms, from weekdays into nights and weekends.

Our eyes now spend much of our waking life focused on screens less than a foot away. Our attention is fragmented by constant alerts, messages, and system demands that masquerade as productivity. This isn't just a quality-of-life issue – it's a capacity issue. Human cognition was never designed for continuous partial attention, perpetual urgency, or endless system friction.

An operating model that requires people to compensate for broken technology with longer hours, constant availability, and heroic effort is not scalable. It doesn't create resilience. It just exhausts it.

Designing for Humans, Not Machines

What if technology worked for humans, rather than the reverse?

Within one of the world's largest global food and agriculture companies that drives over $150B in revenue, a senior operations executive and their team asked that exact question.

The challenge they faced was massive; the company processes millions of orders each year across a fragmented global network of farmers, distributors, and small businesses, many of whom still operate through emails, spreadsheets, PDFs, phone calls, and legacy systems. Each order arrived in a different format, levels of completeness, and degrees of accuracy.

For the company's internal teams, this created daily operational chaos. Customer service representatives spent most of their time copying and pasting information across multiple systems, validating inventory manually, correcting errors, and reconciling inconsistencies between what customers sent and what backend systems required. Errors triggered costly downstream problems – missed shipments, incorrect pricing, delayed deliveries, and fractured customer trust. Scaling the business meant scaling human data entry, not value creation.

Instead of forcing farmers and small shops into complex Electronic Data Interchange systems to make the company's life easier, they reversed the equation by asking, "What if we adapt to our customers instead of making them adapt to us?"

Partnering with Automation Anywhere, the company deployed a Support AI Agent capable of extracting order details from any source – email, phone transcript, or portal – then applying business logic, validating inventory, completing orders, and sending confirmations.

The results were powerful[4]:

- Order processing dropped from 5+ minutes per order, to less than a minute
- 70% of order processing became automated, freeing up customer service reps to better serve customers – not just enter data
- $10–15 million in annual savings were delivered with just one process

More importantly, the employees who were focused on order management stopped living as digital serfs. They were no longer memorizing commands or toggling through screens. They were doing real human work: building customer relationships, solving problems, and understanding their needs.

■ ■ ■

To understand why this kind of redesign matters so deeply, we have to look beyond business metrics and into human cognition itself. NASA developed the Task Load Index (TLX) to measure mental workload in life-or-death environments like piloting spacecraft and aircraft. It quantifies how much strain a system places on the human brain – not in theory, but in measurable physiological and cognitive terms.

NASA's cognitive load metric (TLX) makes the difference clear: poorly designed systems scored a grueling 78.25; well-designed systems scored 29.75.[5] In other words, bad system design can more than double the mental burden on a human being. What NASA learned in space is the same truth most enterprises ignore on Earth; when interfaces are designed for machines instead of for people, performance collapses long before motivation does.

The modern workplace has unintentionally recreated this problem at scale. Smartphones, collaboration tools, and enterprise systems have become always-present interfaces competing for human attention throughout the day. And here's where NASA's lesson becomes personal for most of us: research shows that the mere presence of a smartphone reduces available cognitive capacity, even when the device is turned off. The brain subconsciously allocates processing power to monitor the possibility of interruption – just as a pilot must stay alert to cockpit signals, even when nothing is actively happening.

In effect, we have surrounded knowledge workers with thousands of low-grade "cockpit alerts" layered on top of already poorly designed enterprise systems. The result is a continuous cognitive tax – fragmented attention, rising mental fatigue, and diminished decision quality – not because people are less capable, but because the systems they operate were never designed for sustained human performance.

To escape this trap, we must rethink human-machine collaboration not by asking humans to work harder or stay more connected, but by redesigning systems to reduce cognitive load, respect human limits, and allow people to focus on judgment, creativity, and outcomes rather than constant system management.

We're moving from:

- Command-based interaction ("memorize syntax or fail")
- to graphical interaction (click through menus)
- to intent-based interaction ("tell the system what you want").

You shouldn't need to navigate through technological hurdles like Sarah had to. You should simply say:

"I need the quarterly reports so I can prepare for my 9:00 a.m. meeting."

The system handles the *how*. Humans focus on *the what and the why*.

But before systems can do that for us, humans must temporarily do the work of redesigning systems. Thankfully, we're not starting from zero.

■ ■ ■

There is already a global, rigorously tested framework for this shift. It's one that most enterprises may not be putting into practice.

ISO 9241-210:2019 is the international standard created by the International Organization for Standardization (ISO) to define how human-centered systems should actually be designed. Built on decades of research in ergonomics, cognitive science, and human-computer interaction, it establishes clear principles for reducing cognitive load, aligning systems with human capabilities, and designing technology that supports people.

Despite its unassuming name, ISO 9241-210 is widely referenced and applied in safety-critical and highly regulated industries such as aviation, healthcare, and industrial control, which are domains where design failures cost lives, not just productivity. The irony is hard to miss: We rigorously protect human cognition in cockpits and control rooms yet routinely ignore the same principles in the digital systems millions of knowledge workers use every day.

It lays out a human-centered design approach[6]:

1. Understand real users and their actual needs.
2. Involve them continually during design.
3. Iterate based on real feedback, not imagined behavior.

Stanford school – one of the world's most influential centers for design thinking and human-centered innovation – expands this philosophy to: empathize, define, ideate, prototype, and test.[7]

Standards like ISO 9241-210 make one thing unmistakably clear: Human-centered design cannot stop at interfaces or workflows – it must extend into how work itself is defined, allocated, and executed. Designing better screens or cleaner handoffs helps, but it doesn't solve the deeper problem if humans are still forced to act as translators between systems, exception handlers for brittle logic, or shock absorbers for poorly designed processes. To truly reduce cognitive load, systems must take on more responsibility for reasoning, coordination, and execution – allowing humans to step out of constant system management and back into judgment, creativity, and decision-making. This is where human-centered design stops being a UX philosophy and becomes an operating model for the AI-first enterprise.

■ ■ ■

At Automation Anywhere, we've built on this model with the Referral Agent, which flips how work is defined. Instead of job postings, managers describe the actual tasks and proportions – such as financial analysis, presentations, and stakeholder engagement. The agent asks clarifying questions humans forget, recommends what to automate, and isolates the uniquely human work that remains.

When we tested this with incumbents, the most common question wasn't "Will this replace me?" but "When can this automate the parts of my job I dislike?"

Similarly, the global food and agriculture company we referenced saved $10–15 million annually from reimagining a single process. But the real value wasn't in the cost savings alone. It was in the customer service representatives who were able to automate the parts of the job they didn't enjoy in order to focus more on the aspects of the job that were fulfilling. The value was also in the farmers who could submit orders however they wanted without learning a new technology system, especially when they're already working until sundown. The value in the transformation from humans serving machines to machines serving humans is priceless.

As the company's automation leadership put it, "Far from resting on our automation wins, we're doubling down on innovation. As new technologies emerge, we'll continue refining existing processes and tackling complex, high-value use cases – unlocking even greater impact through the advanced capabilities of Agentic AI."[8]

Technology was never meant to dominate human attention, drain human energy, and dictate human behavior. It was meant to disappear into the background and amplify what only humans can do: judge, create, connect, empathize and decide. The organizations that win in The Five-Year Century will be the ones that reverse this relationship entirely.

The Leader's Playbook: Shifting the Human-Technology Power Dynamics

Leaders who successfully break the illusion of technological servitude don't run better workshops. They redesign power, priorities, and operating mechanics at the top of the enterprise. Here are the five leadership actions that will help your organization end technological servitude.

1. Redefine Success around Cognitive Load, Not System Uptime

Today, systems are considered "successful" if they are stable – even if they exhaust the workforce. Sarah's morning was the result of systems optimized for control, not human performance. Today's leaders should expand enterprise performance metrics to include human cognitive burden, not just availability, latency, and cost.

Leaders should demand visibility into metrics such as:

- Friction per transaction
- Time lost to tool switching
- Stress and rework driven by system design

The ultimate outcome is for productivity to rise through structural improvement.

2. Eliminate "Training as a Strategy" and Replace It with Intent-First Design

In the future operating model, leaders should require that all new enterprise systems prove they can be used with minimal formal training, especially as AI helps make today's technology systems more intuitive.

If a system requires weeks of onboarding to function, the design has already failed. Complex training is no longer a badge of sophistication but is evidence of poor human-machine alignment. The leadership question must shift from: "How do we train people to use this system?" to "Why does this system need training at all?"

The outcome leads to faster adoption, lower resistance to AI, and substantially lower hidden productivity taxes.

3. Make Human Experience a Leading Enterprise Asset

Wouldn't it be great if employee experience was elevated to the same level of fiduciary responsibility as financial capital and data?

Leaders should be asking:

- Which parts of our workforce operate inside constant digital friction?
- Which roles are quietly performing "unpaid system integration" through their own cognitive load?
- Where are we scaling humans to compensate for bad system or process design?

The ultimate outcome should be sustained performance for your employees without increasing any cognitive debt.

4. Mandate AI as a Partner to Employees – Not a New Master

AI that adds dashboards, prompts, escalations, and approvals without removing human burden simply accelerates servitude. In The Five-Year Century, AI must absorb complexity, not multiply it. Top leaders will require all AI deployments to reduce human coordination, navigation, and monitoring – not increase it. The litmus test for every AI initiative must be:

- Does this remove steps – or add them?
- Does this absorb coordination – or create new oversight?
- Does this give humans leverage – or more supervision?

The future of work will not be decided by smarter tools, but by leaders willing to reverse who serves whom. When technology works for humans, performance, dignity, and scale finally move in the same direction.

PART

III

Becoming Future-Ready

8

Designing for Outcomes-Driven Leadership

What We Can Learn from Quarterbacks

Whether a fan of American football or not, and even if the sport is most closely followed in the United States, many people know that the quarterback is an important position. One of the best players at the position is Patrick Mahomes, the multi-championship winning quarterback of the Kansas City Chiefs who is widely considered one of the best players of all-time. When Mahomes and other NFL quarterbacks walk onto the field on Sundays, there is one job: help get the ball in the end zone to put their team in position to win games.

Mahomes doesn't hire his offensive line or skills position players, set their compensation, or manage their career development. Those responsibilities belong to general managers, offensive coordinators, the head coach, and position coaches. Yet Mahomes leads the offense, makes split-second decisions under pressure, and adjusts plays at the line of scrimmage when the defense shows formations the coordinator didn't anticipate. He succeeds through a combination of talent, relentless preparation, and the trust earned through consistent performance.[1]

As one example of his greatness, when Mahomes lost star wide receiver Tyreek Hill to a trade in 2022, a player in his prime who at the time was one of the league's most decorated players, he didn't demand a replacement or complain about inadequate resources. He adapted his entire approach and focused on spreading the ball out to more players. By distributing passes across several different teammates per game, he won back-to-back championships (his second and third titles) with what critics at the time called "limited weapons on offense." The system worked because everyone understood their role: The general manager built a deep roster, the coaches developed the talent, and the quarterback executed the plays alongside the team.

An NFL roster turns over by 56% annually. Over a two-year span, over 65% of the team can look entirely different. And yet, high-performing quarterbacks maintain excellence by building chemistry rapidly and adapting to whoever shows up on game day.[2] This separation of concerns creates remarkable agility.

There are similar examples to the NFL quarterback in other sports in various parts of the world. The specific sport is not the point, but rather the fast-moving nature of competitive games and how successful teams organize themselves to win.

Most enterprises operate nothing like this even though winning is just as paramount.

■ ■ ■

In most cases, organizations optimize for control, predictability, and efficiency through hierarchical command structures. These pyramids worked when markets moved slowly, expertise concentrated at the top, and coordination costs justified centralized decision-making. However, the world has changed.

Recent research clarifies what separates winners from losers. Boston Consulting Group studied AI-first organizations and identified core traits that define the emerging model of companies.

1. These organizations demonstrate wider competitive moats through brand and intellectual property, expanding advantages that matter while reducing reliance on operational scale that AI eliminates.

2. They operate with reshaped P&L models, where technology becomes one of the largest cost categories – often at levels that would be unsustainable for traditionally structured competitors.
3. They've built decentralized technology foundations where business units lead adoption rather than waiting for centralized IT mandates.[3]
4. Their operating models streamline AI workflows from the ground up, treating intelligent systems as core drivers rather than supplementary tools.
5. They employ materially fewer people per dollar of revenue, while paying significant premiums for the most scarce, high-impact talent.

What makes these transformation traits possible? The answer lies in a few simple shifts: organizing around outcomes rather than functions; expertise rather than hierarchy; and results rather than reporting relationships.

The quarterback model is one example of an outcomes-focused organization in practice. Outcome owners focus exclusively on achievement without managing people. They make tactical decisions in compressed timeframes rather than seeking approvals through hierarchical chains. They succeed through expertise and influence, rather than positional authority.

Organizations embracing similar structures unlock speed that hierarchies cannot match. AI-first organizations can operate with significantly higher revenue per employee compared to traditional structures, proving that alternative models work at scale.[4] The performance gap compounds daily. Leaders reinvest AI-generated savings into further AI capabilities, creating advantage loops that competitors pursuing incremental change cannot close.

■　■　■

The way a company organizes itself directly affects the speed at which information flows, the integrity of the data as it moves within an org chart, and the ultimate quality of the organization's responsiveness to market demands. Unfortunately, for most companies, there is a mismatch between environmental demands and structural capabilities. Most organizations remain locked in structures that require weeks for decisions, months for resource reallocation, and several quarters for strategic pivots. This strict, linear flow of authority represents an existential threat to companies that cannot keep pace with change.

Consider what happens when a customer need emerges that cuts across departmental boundaries. In traditional organizations, for a leader to identify the right expertise for a task, they must navigate org charts and personal networks. Assembling a team requires approval from upper managers, each of whom protects their turf and headcount. Coordinating work across functions creates meetings where people defend departmental priorities rather than optimizing for larger customer outcomes. By the time the team forms and begins work, the opportunity has often passed to a more agile competitor.

These aren't bugs in the system. They're features of hierarchical design, working exactly as intended to maximize control at the expense of speed.

The costs compound in ways that financial statements don't capture. Breakthrough ideas die in approval processes before reaching anyone with the authority to say yes. Strong customer insight gets filtered out as information travels up layers. Talented employees leave because they feel that their overly engineered roles restrict their capabilities.

Technology was supposed to solve many of these problems. Email, texts and WhatsApp replaced old-school memo routing, Zoom meetings made it easier to stay connected across the globe, and collaboration software made editing and sharing work easier across teams. Yet somehow, these tools have continued to magnify hierarchical constraints. Many communication tools – like it or not – simply enable more meetings, more approval requests, and more activities or status updates that take away from a focus on outcomes. The digital logs create permanent records that can make people afraid to make the wrong decision or provide critical feedback.

Incremental reforms to hierarchical structures are often presented as pragmatic solutions, but in reality, they reinforce the very constraints they claim to fix. Organizations add "cross-functional teams" that still report into functional managers who evaluate performance based on departmental priorities, not outcomes. They create "agile pods" that appear autonomous on paper but still require director or VP approval before making any consequential decision. They implement "matrix structures" that give employees two or three bosses instead of one, often multiplying coordination costs, diffusing accountability, and slowing execution even further.

These incremental changes fail because they try to reconcile two incompatible goals: preserving hierarchical control while claiming to enable speed and autonomy. The result is an organization that talks about empowerment but structurally prevents it.

So, what would it take to build organizations that optimize for speed and adaptability? The answer may be found in nature.

Nature's Proof of Concept: Project Beehive

Skeptics of outcome-focused structures argue that coordination without hierarchy might work in theory but fails at scale. Someone must be in charge to make final decisions, break ties, and maintain accountability when thousands of individuals need direction. However, biological systems that have operated for 150 million years prove these objections wrong.

Take honeybees, for example. Honeybee colonies coordinate 10,000 to 60,000 "autonomous individuals" through distributed signals and dynamic role shifts, accomplishing tasks that require extraordinary levels of coordination, resilience, and speed at mass scale.

The queen bee occupies a powerful place in human imagination – as a ruler, commander, or CEO of the hive. This is not just inaccurate; it is a projection of human hierarchy onto a system that does not use it. In reality, the queen exercises no managerial or operational authority whatsoever. She produces eggs and emits pheromones that signal colony health and cohesion – but she does not direct work, assign roles, set priorities, or make decisions about foraging locations, comb construction, or resource allocation.[5]

Those decisions are made continuously by the colony itself. The organizational chart humans imagine with the queen at the apex issuing commands does not exist. It exists only in our hierarchically conditioned minds.

Worker bees switch roles autonomously in response to colony needs, a behavior called age polytheism. The typical progression moves bees from safe internal work to dangerous external tasks over their five- to seven week lifespans. Days zero to two: cleaning cells. Days three to ten: nursing larvae. Days ten to twenty: building honeycomb and processing food. Days twenty-one onward: foraging outside the hive.[6]

Crucially, this is not a rigid career ladder. This schedule flexes when colony survival demands it. Researchers created colonies using only bees of the same age. Some individuals began foraging at just four to seven days old, three weeks earlier than normal. Others delayed transitions.[7] If you remove all foragers from a colony, bees as young as four days old become precocious foragers to fill the gap. Hormonal and neural systems adjust in real time to support these shifts.

The lesson is not about obedience, but adaptability. Rapid collective response to changing conditions matters more than fixed roles or perfect individual optimization.

These systems, in which outcomes dictate structure rather than structure dictating outcomes, operate through quorum-based decision-making. High-quality decisions emerge from many independent evaluations coordinated through simple, transparent signals.

For example, when bee swarms seek new homes, approximately 500 scout bees independently evaluate potential locations. They perform waggle dances indicating the quality of the location.[8] Scouts returning from high-quality sites perform longer, more vigorous dances than those returning from inferior sites. No bee compares all options, no central planner aggregates the data, and no authority issues a final decree.

Rather, a decision for a new home emerges through cross-inhibition. Scouts visiting different sites deliver stop signals to dancers advertising competing locations. Once 30 to 40 scouts gather at a single site, the quorum threshold is reached, and the swarm commits to the location as their new home. Consensus is achieved without command from the queen. Coordination emerges without control from any individual.[9]

To some, this example may seem impossible for a human organization, but it happens already to some degree in startups and within smaller teams elsewhere. It should happen a lot more in the future. In the age of AI, a group of people, united by purpose and ambition and armed with hundreds of AI agents, will be able to figure out a path forward to achieve accelerated outcomes.

■   ■   ■

At Automation Anywhere, we've built an organizational model called Project Beehive that aims to bring these AI-first design principles to life. The initiative redesigns how leadership works by transitioning from traditional people managers to a dynamic, project-led structure. Project Beehive empowers individuals to lead based on expertise rather than hierarchy, following a model where outcome owners focus on execution without managing people's careers or compensation. The structure centralizes HR services and employment decisions, removing conflicts of interest that plague traditional management roles. AI agents provide on-demand training and coaching rather than scheduled quarterly reviews. The anticipated results mirror what honeybee colonies achieve: greater agility through rapid team formation, better talent utilization by matching expertise to needs regardless of organizational boundaries, stronger alignment with employee interests by enabling people to contribute where they add most value, and a culture built on collaboration rather than territorial competition.[10]

The critical difference between insect colonies and human organizations is that humans can consciously design better systems rather than relying on evolution to discover them over millions of years. We can create transparent systems that make the organizational state visible to everyone. We can build AI agents that signal where expertise is needed. We can design incentive structures aligning individual interests with collective outcomes. We can implement feedback mechanisms that surface problems early rather than allowing them to compound.

Biological evidence shows that coordination without hierarchy works at a massive scale. The question is whether organizations will learn from millions of years of evolutionary optimization or continue believing that hierarchical structures invented barely a century ago are the ideal way to organize human effort.

Project Beehive is not a metaphor. It is an operating model whose time has arrived. But if the destination is now clear, the harder question remains unanswered: *Why do so few organizations manage to get there?*

To answer that, we must confront the invisible structures that keep companies trapped in the past.

The Architecture That Makes Change Possible

Companies rarely fail because they lack intelligence, technology, or ambition. They often fail because of invisible architecture – psychological, cognitive, and political – that shapes how people actually behave day to day and quietly overrides strategy. A few forces lock organizations into rigidity even when leaders attempt to design for flexibility:

- The absence of real psychological safety for role mobility (the ability to move between teams, initiatives, or responsibilities without penalty)
- Cognitive biases that distort how teams form and how talent is evaluated and deployed
- Management roles that contain built-in conflicts of interest between optimizing for enterprise outcomes and protecting local headcount, status, or control

Each of these forces works independently. Together, they make structural change appear active on paper but performative instead of real.

■ ■ ■

Let's look at the importance of psychological safety, for example. Research by Amy Edmondson has revealed an interesting dynamic through studying medical teams. Higher-performing surgical units reported more errors than lower-performing units, a finding that initially seemed paradoxical.[11] But in light of dynamics on psychologically safe teams, the explanation proved straightforward: high-performing teams created environments where discussing mistakes felt safe, so errors got surfaced, analyzed, and corrected early, before they compounded into systemic failure. Low-performing teams punished people who admitted errors, so mistakes stayed hidden until they caused patient harm. The units that appeared to have fewer errors had more; they simply lacked the psychological safety to surface them and learn from them.[12]

The lesson transfers directly to enterprise transformation. What actually creates psychological safety is not soft culture work, but leadership behavior reinforced by systems that make speaking up rational, not risky. Edmondson's research consistently points to a short list of drivers:

- Leaders who model vulnerability by admitting their own limitations
- Teams that respond to mistakes with curiosity rather than blame

- Environments where asking for help is seen as a strength rather than a weakness and does not negatively affect performance reviews or career trajectories
- Organizational systems that reward learning rather than punish failure through incentives, promotion criteria, and resource allocation

Each of the above factors requires leaders to behave in ways that feel counterintuitive to executives trained in hierarchical cultures, where admitting uncertainty may be seen as a sign of weakness or loss of authority. That's why it's so critical that before implementing any "Project Beehive" style transformations, organizations must first engineer environments where interpersonal risk is survivable and visibly survivable to others. Without that foundation, flexible structures don't produce agility but risk leading to paralysis as employees rationally retreat to self-protection instead of enterprise contribution.

■ ■ ■

Beyond the psychological safety barrier, cognitive biases compound coordination challenges. Human cognition evolved for small groups where individuals knew everyone personally, collaboration happened face-to-face, and reputation information traveled through direct observation and social networks. These evolutionary features restrict team adaptability and flexibility in environments with hundreds or thousands of strangers. The reasons lie in proximity and affiliation bias.

Proximity and affiliation bias leads people to collaborate with physically nearby colleagues or favor known colleagues over strangers with superior capabilities, rather than seeking optimal expertise. When problems arise, people ask the person they are most comfortable with rather than seeking out whoever in the organization best understands the issue. When projects form, managers select from teams they interact with daily rather than scanning the entire talent pool. Employees volunteer for projects where they know the leaders rather than projects where their skills would add the most value. This makes psychological sense, working with people you can walk up to or have worked with on a previous project makes things easier than coordinating across time zones and organizational boundaries. However, it systematically underutilizes distributed expertise and often creates local optimums that perform worse than global optimums would.

Again, this seems rational and sound at the individual level. Working with trusted colleagues reduces coordination costs and interpersonal risk. On the other hand, it can create systematic talent misallocation where familiarity matters more than capability.

Project Beehive's value proposition specifically addresses these limitations: AI agents can provide rosters of who should be on the field quarterbacking each outcome, eliminating biases that constrain human team formation. AI agents can help track thousands of employees across multiple dimensions that humans cannot hold in working memory, current skills and expertise levels, developing capabilities that aren't yet reflected in job titles, interests and aspirations that might motivate high performance, availability and current workload capacity, past performance on similar projects, and collaboration patterns that predict team chemistry. When combined, information advantage finally makes expertise-based team formation feasible rather than theoretical.

What makes AI-enabled team formation powerful isn't that it replaces human judgment or removes managers from talent decisions. It supports and augments human judgment by surfacing options that proximity and affiliation biases would otherwise filter out. Instead of a manager selecting from the dozen people they know well, AI-enabled systems expand the decision set, allowing leaders to select from the hundreds who possess relevant expertise. Instead of employees having to wonder how to find projects that align with their interests, systems can proactively surface opportunities that match capabilities while leaving final participation decisions with people and leaders. Instead of expertise sitting idle because no one knows it exists, organizations can make capabilities visible and actionable, enabling leaders to deploy talent fluidly where it creates the most value.

This technological capability matters now because the 40% productivity gains that demographic mathematics demand won't come from making existing teams slightly more efficient. They'll come from better matching expertise to needs, reducing coordination friction, and enabling people to contribute wherever they add most value rather than wherever organizational boundaries place them – with AI acting as a decision-support layer, not an autonomous talent manager.

■   ■   ■

Looking further into the challenges with traditional management structures, a manager role combines three distinct functions that create systematic conflicts of interest: executing work through direct reports, making employment decisions about compensation and career progression, and developing people through coaching and skill building. Each of these functions is legitimate and valuable on its own, but their combination, especially when concentrated in a single role, creates systemic tensions. This combination of functions, each of which is susceptible to human biases, undermines the utility of the manager's role in light of the greater organization's objectives when the enterprise needs speed, flexibility, and cross-boundary collaboration.

Consider performance evaluation. When managers simultaneously evaluate performance and coach development, employees become reluctant to surface limitations that might affect ratings. The coaching relationship requires vulnerability and admission of weaknesses. The evaluation relationship creates incentives to hide flaws and emphasize strengths. Asking one person to play the roles of both coach and judge guarantees a conflict of interest – not because managers lack skill or intent, but because the structure itself makes trust fragile.

Resource allocation presents similar dilemmas. Managers control headcount budgets and compensation pools for their teams. When outcome-focused work requires expertise from outside the team, managers must decide whether to "loan" their people to other priorities, potentially impacting their own team's deliverables and metrics. The rational manager hoards talent even when organizational priorities would benefit from fluid reallocation – a behavior driven by incentive design, not personal greed. This creates the "talent stuck in silos" problem that leaders complain about while maintaining the management structures that guarantee it.

Career progression compounds the issue further. In hierarchical organizations, advancement typically means managing people. This converts excellent individual contributors into mediocre managers, taking them away from work they do well, and putting them into roles they may never master. The organization loses high-performing contributors and gains low-performing managers, not because management is unimportant, but because it is treated as the default path rather than a distinct professional discipline. As Nancy jokes, "I've been trying to turn good workers into good managers for over 40 years, and I've succeeded maybe three percent of the time. So, I'm just going to stop trying."

Project Beehive proposes a different architecture, separating employment decisions from day-to-day execution, centralizing HR services around compensation and career development, using AI agents for training and coaching that's available on demand rather than scheduled quarterly, and deploying expert human support based on what teams need rather than reporting relationships. This model does not remove managers; it reframes their role away from gatekeeping and administration toward leadership, judgment, and enablement. This doesn't eliminate the human element. It focuses human attention on activities that matter, like real-time strategic direction-setting, culture-building, relationship development, and expertise application rather than administrative overhead and coordination maintenance.

In this sense, humans act as quarterbacks for outcomes – setting direction, reading context, and making consequential decisions – while AI handles much of the coordination, pattern detection, and routine execution that previously consumed managerial bandwidth.

Resistance to this model typically centers on three objections.

- First, employees need someone responsible for their careers who knows them personally. This assumes career development requires knowing someone for years rather than having systems that match capabilities to opportunities based on data. This also overlooks the continued role of human mentors, sponsors, and leaders in helping people interpret those opportunities and make meaningful choices.
- Second, that coordination requires managers to negotiate resource allocation. This assumes informal negotiations among

managers produce better results than transparent systems that allocate based on priorities and capabilities.

- Third, that performance evaluation requires a manager's judgment. This assumes manager judgment provides a more accurate assessment than a combination of outcome measurement, peer feedback, and AI analysis of work patterns. In practice, the strongest assessments emerge from combining human judgment with richer, more objective signals.

Each objection reflects reasonable concerns while defending practices that create systematic biases. The question isn't whether traditional management provides any value. Many managers do. The question is around how to maximize the value provided by a human manager given the constraints identified. The evidence increasingly suggests that alternative models could help improve results.

Delivering an AI-First Enterprise

Traditional organizational structures cannot deliver the 40% productivity improvements required for the future. They have already been optimized for decades, and the remaining gains are marginal. The only viable path to the next order of performance runs through organizational redesign – eliminating coordination friction, deploying expertise fluidly based on needs rather than boundaries, and allowing systems to absorb work that unnecessarily consumes human attention.

Boston Consulting Group's research on AI-first organizations makes this performance gap visible.[13] Companies that fully redesign processes around AI achieve materially higher revenue per employee than traditional enterprises. These are not hypothetical models. They are operating companies serving real customers in competitive markets. While the multiplier varies by industry, the pattern is consistent: AI-first operating models unlock performance improvements that incremental structural reforms simply cannot reach.

What follows is not a transformation program or a multi-year roadmap. It is a practical way for leaders to begin shifting how work actually gets done in an AI-first enterprise.

1. Start by Making Outcomes Explicit and Visible

The foundation of an AI-first enterprise is not just technology; it is clarity. Teams cannot self-organize, and systems cannot assist intelligently, if outcomes are vague or hidden inside strategy decks.

Leaders must define a small number of outcomes that matter now – not 10, not 20, but a few that represent real enterprise priorities. These outcomes should be visible to everyone, along with their current status, deadlines, owners, and known constraints. This shared field of play replaces rumor, escalation, and guesswork with alignment.

When outcomes are explicit, people no longer need to navigate org charts to decide where to contribute. They can see what matters and act accordingly.

2. Make Expertise and Capacity Legible Across the Organization

Once outcomes are visible, the next constraint is almost always talent opacity. Most organizations have no reliable way to see where expertise actually lives, who has capacity, or who wants to work on what next. Decisions default to proximity and familiarity rather than capability.

AI-first enterprises address this by creating transparent systems that surface expertise, availability, and constraints across boundaries. When outcome owners need specific capabilities, systems can identify and connect them with people who possess relevant skills, regardless of where they sit in the formal hierarchy. When employees want to contribute to high-priority initiatives, they can discover opportunities without relying on personal networks or permission chains.

Managers remain critical here – not as gatekeepers, but as validators. They help assess fit, sequence commitments, resolve conflicts, and ensure that ambition does not outrun capacity. The result is better talent utilization, faster execution, and less wasted human potential.

3. Replace Approval Chains with Clear Decision Guardrails

Resistance to flatter, outcome-driven structures often stems from fear of losing control. That fear is understandable, but something to work through.

AI-first organizations do not eliminate governance. They replace approval chains with clear decision frameworks. Teams are given explicit authority to act within defined thresholds, with escalation reserved for the few decisions that truly require senior judgment.

This shift is subtle but powerful. When people know what they can decide, how much they can spend, and where the red lines are, they move faster and with more confidence. Governance becomes an enabling system rather than a bottleneck. Just as importantly, innovation stays in the open instead of being driven underground by opaque restrictions.

4. Use AI as a Signaling System, Not a Command System

AI systems excel at what humans cannot do at scale: continuously monitoring flow, detecting patterns, and signaling when conditions change. In an AI-first enterprise, these systems function much like pheromones in a beehive – indicating where attention, expertise, or intervention is needed.

When outcome dashboards show that a critical initiative lacks capacity, AI systems can surface the gap. When teams report blockers, systems can route the right support. When work completes and capacity frees up, that availability becomes immediately visible rather than trapped in quarterly planning cycles.

But AI does not replace leadership. Leaders interpret signals, weigh tradeoffs, arbitrate conflicts, and decide when judgment – not automation – must prevail. The system accelerates awareness; humans retain accountability.

5. Redefine Leadership Around Leverage, Not Coordination

As teams organize around outcomes and systems handle more coordination, the role of leaders does not diminish – it concentrates.

Leaders set direction. They define what outcomes matter and why. They establish the decision frameworks that guide action at the edges. They build cultures where psychological safety enables experimentation rather than risk avoidance. They mentor, absorb risk on behalf of their teams, and remain accountable when outcomes fall short. This is strategic work that creates leverage, not tactical work that consumes time.

In this model, leaders function like quarterbacks – reading the field, calling plays, and deciding when to rely on AI and automation and when to override them. Their teams and AI agents execute. Leadership is amplified, not displaced.

6. Always Stay Human-Focused

None of this transformation is easy. People who have built careers in stable roles must adapt to environments where continuous change is the norm. At the same time, organizations must recognize that asking people to move faster requires better systems, clearer direction, and stronger leadership – not less of it.

The AI-first enterprise is not built by removing humans from the loop. It is built by redesigning the loop so that human judgment is applied where it creates the most value, and machine intelligence handles the rest.

Great leadership has always mattered. In an AI-first enterprise, it matters even more. We will always need great quarterbacks.

9

The Age of Personalization

The Rise and Fall of Standardization

What if we could take the best parts of consumer experience and work in the pre-industrial age and scale them for our future? Let's show you what that means. We don't have to look back too far.

Savile Row, London, 1969. A master tailor at Henry Poole & Co. – the firm that's been dressing British aristocracy since the Napoleonic era – hunches over a length of superfine wool. He'll spend the next 80+ hours transforming this fabric into a single custom suit, placing every stitch with the precision of a neurosurgeon who cares deeply about lapel width.[1]

His client, meanwhile, will endure three to six fittings, each lasting 20 to 60 minutes of standing still while someone circles them with pins and chalk, muttering measurements in a dialect that predates modern English.[2] The price tag? A bespoke suit could cost the equivalent of a major purchase – often comparable to a modest new car in that era – paid not just for fabric, but for time, fittings, and craft.[3]

Hand-stitched tailoring still commands a premium today, precisely because it represents craftsmanship, quality, and human artistry that some customers actively seek out. For those who value the premium nature, the time and cost are worth the investment. But what made Savile Row or other luxury designers exceptional was never meant to be the default for everyone. It was personalization as privilege, not personalization at scale.

Walk into a tech-enabled tailoring shop today and an AI-powered body scanner captures countless measurements with little margin of error.[4] For customers who don't even have time for that, they can pull out their phone, snap a few photos, and a mobile app will generate custom measurements in under 60 seconds.[5] A perfectly fitted suit arrives in three to four weeks, at a fraction of the traditional cost.[6]

Even Savile Row itself embraces this transformation. The Eco-Luxe Project now converts wool off-cuts into new luxury cloth, while the London Academy of Bespoke at 27 Savile Row ensures centuries-old craft meets modern sustainability.[7] Tradition and innovation aren't opposites, but partners in creating something better.

So now we must ask: If we can make clothing fit perfectly for millions of different bodies using AI and automation, what can we do for customers, patients and even our own employees?

This question sits at the heart of two parallel transformations happening at once: the personalization of customer experiences and the personalization of human work itself.

■   ■   ■

Let's look at an example from a leading cloud-based human capital and benefits services provider that helps people access and manage their health, wealth, and well-being benefits. The company supports more than 35 million individuals across approximately 4,300 enterprise clients globally, including a majority of Fortune 100 organizations.[8] Every year during open enrollment season, employees depend on this provider to help them navigate one of the most consequential financial decisions they'll make: choosing the right healthcare coverage, retirement contributions, and wellness benefits for their families.

The challenge the company faced is staggering in its complexity. They process 20 million claims annually, six million of which had to be handled manually by over 200 staff members. Every client has different eligibility rules, different plan designs, and different compliance requirements. The receipts and documentation come in every imaginable format. Nothing is standardized. The old systems couldn't handle the variability, leading to endless delays, increased risk of human error, and over 500,000 customer inquiry calls each year. People calling to ask: "Where's my reimbursement? Why was my claim denied? Can someone just tell me what's happening?"[9]

The process was slow, costly, and unsustainable at scale. Something had to change.

At first glance, this is a story about customer experience, with faster reimbursements, fewer calls, and clearer communication. But it's also a clear example of how customer personalization inevitably forces internal work to become personalized as well.

As you will soon see, the company's transformation shows what happens when experiences and processes become customized. When technology handles what technology does best, humans can do what humans do best. And everyone – employees, customers, and shareholders – wins.

■ ■ ■

In the early twentieth century, standardization was revolutionary. It was the saving grace many companies needed to scale what worked. Companies discovered they could dramatically reduce costs through standardization – same products, same processes, same everything. Consequently, workers became extensions of machines. Success wasn't measured by individual satisfaction or creativity, but by how many identical units rolled off the line.

In a short amount of time, this industrial logic infected everything about work. We started writing job descriptions like specifications for machine parts: "Must be able to lift 50 pounds and tolerate fluorescent lighting." We forgot to add "must be impervious to soul-crushing monotony," but perhaps that was implied. Everyone worked 9-to-5, regardless of whether they were morning larks or night owls. We created identical benefits packages, assuming everyone lived in a 1950s nuclear family – working dad, stay-at-home mom, 2.5 kids, and a dog named Spot.

For companies on the cutting edge, though, the switch back to customized practices has been sudden and impactful. For example, in the world of construction – supposedly the ultimate standardized industry – ICON Technologies started 3D-printing homes in Texas. Yes, they replicate standard designs faster, but they also expanded their capabilities to adapt to specific customer needs at scale. They offered curved walls, organic shapes, and personalized floor plans that would have been impossible with traditional methods. Their Wolf Ranch development near Georgetown sold 95 custom homes, each uniquely configured, at prices competitive with cookie-cutter construction – $430,000 to $599,000.[10] Not to mention that the construction time was three times faster, and material costs were cut by nearly a third.[11]

In manufacturing, Xometry transformed custom parts production from a weeks-long quoting nightmare into instant pricing through AI. Their platform connects over 68,000 buyers with over 4,400 suppliers globally, each order customized yet delivered faster than traditional batch production. Revenue hit $545.6 million in 2024, growing 23% year-over-year.[12]

Even insurance – perhaps the most standardized industry of all – has cracked. Progressive's Snapshot program analyzes actual driving behavior instead of demographic proxies. Safe drivers save an average of $231 at renewal. Some save up to $322.[13] The usage-based insurance market will reach $70.46 billion by 2030.[14] Finally, how you actually drive matters more than your ZIP code.

The cracks in standardization's sustainability have been on display since the 1990s. Remember when coffee was just coffee? That was, until Starbucks started offering tens of thousands of drink combinations. Dell started letting customers build computers to order, and the desire for bespoke products went mainstream when Nike launched Nike By You which let people design their own shoes.[15]

These shifts in the 90s were not novel ideas. Stan Davis coined "mass customization" in 1987.[16] B. Joseph Pine II followed the train of thought in 1993 with a framework that made CFOs' hearts sing: "Low unit costs of mass production plus flexibility of individual customization."[17] Four approaches were identified: Collaborative, Adaptive, Cosmetic, and Transparent. Unfortunately, since implementing these ideas was complex and expensive, they were doomed to consultant speak purgatory for the next three decades. Until, finally, AI came along to make things easier.

■   ■   ■

The shift that must happen now is for business leaders to apply personalization principles to both serving their customers and enhancing their organizational structure.

This is where the case study of the human capital and benefits services provider becomes instructive. Leadership within the company's AI and automation team was facing a problem that couldn't be solved by hiring more people. They had 200-plus staff members, who were skilled professionals with college degrees and years of experience, spending their days manually processing claims. It was the same routine over and over, checking receipts, validating eligibility, entering data and authorizing the claim, etc.

The company's employees could order anything on Amazon and have it arrive the next day. They could deposit checks by taking a photo. They expected instant everything in their personal lives, and of course they knew their customers did as well. Then they came to work and spent eight hours processing the same routine claims that took too long to deliver customer satisfaction. It took days to complete what should take hours. The system designed to help people navigate their benefits was making everyone's life harder – employees and customers alike.

Leadership of the AI and automation team realized the company faced an existential challenge. Workers with choices could leave for more meaningful, less cumbersome work. Customers with expectations shaped by Amazon, Netflix and DoorDash would demand better, more personalized service. The company's manual approach was becoming obsolete in a world where "instant and personalized" had become the baseline. Making the old way slightly faster wouldn't be enough.

The Economic Inevitability of Personalization

For most of modern business history, personalization was expensive by definition. Tailoring experiences to individual needs meant more labor, more handoffs, more exceptions, and more cost. Standardization scaled, customization did not.

That trade-off is now breaking down – not because people suddenly value personalization more, but because three structural forces have inverted the economics.

First, AI can recognize patterns at a scale no human ever could. Consider Netflix, which analyzes viewing behavior across more than 325 million subscribers in over 190 countries. The system has identified tens of thousands of micro-genres and continuously adapts recommendations at the individual level. The result is not just a better user experience but a measurable economic outcome: roughly 80% of viewing comes from personalized recommendations, translating into an estimated $1 billion or more in annual value retention. What once required editorial teams and manual curation now happens continuously, algorithmically, and at marginal cost.[18]

Another useful example is Spotify. Its personalization engine does more than increase listening time. It reshapes how artists are discovered, how long-tail content finds audiences, and how value accrues across the ecosystem. Importantly, Spotify also illustrates the boundary conditions: personalization works because humans still define goals, ethics, and creative direction. Algorithms optimize *within* those constraints; they do not replace them.

Second, the infrastructure required for personalization has democratized. Previously, you needed Amazon-level resources to deliver personalization. Today, those same capabilities are increasingly embedded in SaaS platforms. In logistics, companies like ShipBob allow mid-market e-commerce brands to offer personalized fulfillment by routing orders dynamically across distributed warehouses based on customer location, demand patterns, and inventory constraints. One customer, Makesy, reduced shipping times by roughly two-thirds while managing thousands of SKUs. The key shift is structural, and personalization is no longer built from scratch; it's rented, modular, and operationally lightweight.[19]

Third, personalization scales precisely because humans do not. We have cognitive limits. Dunbar's number suggests we can maintain around 150 stable social relationships; in practice, most people struggle to track even a fraction of that in a professional context related to preferences, constraints, goals, and histories. AI systems have no such limitations. They do not forget past interactions, they do not tire of exception handling, and they improve as variability increases. At scale, this flips the old model: standardization becomes the bottleneck, not personalization.

While personalization first became visible through customer-facing experiences – recommendations, pricing, fulfillment, care – it does not stop at the consumer boundary.

Healthcare provides one of the clearest illustrations of personalization moving from consumer experiences to larger necessity. A large US healthcare provider working with Automation Anywhere used

AI-powered document automation and intelligent workflows to personalize patient intake, prior authorization, and care coordination. Rather than forcing every patient through identical administrative pathways, the system adapted to individual clinical profiles, insurance requirements, and treatment plans – automatically routing cases based on medical urgency, payer rules, and patient history. Routine cases moved through in hours instead of days, while complex cases were flagged early and directed to specialized clinical and administrative teams. The impact wasn't just operational efficiency; it reduced care delays, lowered administrative burden on clinicians, and improved patient care and satisfaction by ensuring people received the *right* level of attention at the *right* moment. This is the power of personalization when it matters most.

Take all of this together, and it's easy to see why the broader personalization market is projected to grow from roughly $460 billion in the early 2020s to more than $700 billion over the next decade.[20] These aren't incremental improvements. They're exponential transformations.

■ ■ ■

For the human capital and benefits services provider, instead of trying to standardize the chaos by forcing hundreds of different rule sets into one rigid process, their AI and automation team asked a more interesting question: What if the system could absorb variation – so people didn't have to behave like machines?

The turning point came through a series of collaborative design workshops that brought together the frontline teams who process claims every day. Rather than abstracting the work from afar, the company worked directly with the people closest to the complexity. Together, they simplified hundreds of overlapping rules into a single, shared standard that software could interpret and apply consistently.[21]

From there, the company deployed Automation Anywhere alongside cloud-based AI services that could read and understand claims documents much like a human would – extracting key information, checking submissions for completeness, identifying exceptions, and automatically handling the routine cases. Only the truly complex or ambiguous claims were routed to human experts for judgment and review.

The result wasn't just faster processing, but a system designed around human strengths. AI handled the scale and variability; people focused on nuance, empathy, and decision-making where it actually mattered.

Processing time dropped from three days to less than one. The system also got smarter. Every claim was handled according to its specific characteristics, with AI learning from each decision to improve subsequent decisions. Routine cases flow through instantly, and complex cases get routed to the right human expert based on the specific type of complexity involved.[22]

Call volume was cut in half because customers no longer needed to call as much. When your claim is processed in hours instead of days, when you get automatic updates through your preferred channel, when the system remembers your history and anticipates your questions, you don't need to pick up the phone. The transformation had achieved its goals in alleviating customer friction and making work more meaningful for employees, while checking the boxes on multiple leadership imperatives such as reducing cost and enhancing culture.

Delivering on the Personalization Revolution

In many sectors, when personalization is applied thoughtfully, productivity and outcomes tend to improve – not because personalization is always magical, but because it aligns decisions more closely with real-world variation.

In agriculture, Climate FieldView analyzes data from hundreds of thousands of test plots, soil conditions, weather patterns, and yield outcomes to generate field-level planting and input recommendations. Rather than treating an entire farm as a single unit, these prescriptions adjust seed selection and density by zone. Studies and grower reports suggest gains of roughly five to eight bushels per acre in many use cases, which is meaningful in a business where margins are thin and variability determines profitability.[23]

In healthcare, Geisinger's MyCode initiative has performed genomic screening on over 325,000 participants. They've identified over 5,100 individuals with previously undetected genetic risks for serious but preventable conditions. That's personalization not as convenience, but for shifting care from reactive, one-size-fits-all treatment toward targeted prevention where intervention matters most.[24]

Even consumer products demonstrate the same pattern. Coca-Cola's Freestyle machines offer 100-plus combinations while streaming preference data back to headquarters. Locations with these machines have reported mid-single-digit sales increases and successful product launches that were informed by consumer behavior, such as with Sprite Cherry and Orange Vanilla Coke.[25]

What links these examples is not the industry, but the mechanism: systems that sense individual variation and respond dynamically outperform systems designed around averages. This has significant competitive implications. Once a company starts personalizing, it can build proprietary datasets that compound its advantage. That said, personalization is not automatic or universal. It requires clean data, thoughtful design, and clear boundaries between automation and human judgment. Poorly implemented personalization can add noise rather than clarity. But when done well, it becomes a structural advantage that deepens a competitive moat over time.

■ ■ ■

Many organizations often stop short of fully delivering on the personalization revolution. They may have begun to personalize relentlessly for customers but expect their own people to conform to standardized roles, schedules, tools, and career paths. Beyond offering personalization to meet the needs of your market, it is equally critical to offer personalization within the workforce itself if an organization expects to succeed with an AI-first operating model.

The human capital and benefits services provider discovered this firsthand during its implementation. Notably, the same systems that enabled personalized customer experiences also enabled personalized work. The infrastructure didn't change; the lens did.

They discovered that different teams experience "good work" very differently. Customer service representatives needed real-time visibility into claim status to answer questions confidently. Finance teams needed clear audit trails and traceability to meet regulatory requirements.

Operations teams needed early warning signals and exception reports to keep work flowing. Rather than forcing every role into a single standardized interface, the company invested in a flexible foundation that could adapt workflows, views, and priorities based on how each group actually worked.[26]

The transformation succeeded because leadership empowered teams to redesign their own workflows. "We didn't impose changes from above," the AI and automation leader explained. "We asked teams to show us what would make their work better, then built technology to enable it."[27]

Here's what this looks like tactically at three levels:

- **Individual Leadership Level:** Document your own optimal patterns of work. When are you most focused? When do you tend to struggle? Use AI tools to adapt meeting schedules, preparation, communication, and task flow to your natural rhythms. Share what works – not as a mandate, but as a signal that individuality is valued. In an AI-first organization, leaders model the future by treating their careers as evolving systems, not static roles. Or, as Nancy tells her team: *"Be weird. It's working for me."*
- **Team Level:** Run small "personalization pilots" that allow teams to experiment with different ways of achieving the same outcomes. Measure results – speed, quality, engagement – not whether everyone followed the same process. Encourage teams to articulate *why* their approach works for them and make those insights visible to others. Over time, this builds psychological safety and reinforces that having a point of view is an asset, not a risk.
- **Organizational Level:** Invest in shared infrastructure that supports personalization at scale – modular systems, role-based views, flexible workflows, and AI tools that adapt to users rather than the reverse. Train leaders to think in terms of enabling patterns instead of enforcing consistency. Most importantly, align incentives, reward managers who unlock diverse strengths and multiply individual impact, rather than those who optimize for sameness and control.

The transformation will not be seamless for many. The benefits, however, significantly outweigh the potential drawbacks. Imagine every individual operating at their peak, an abundance of talent replacing scarcity, and work transforming into an enjoyable pursuit for nearly every team member.

At Automation Anywhere, we're seeing 55% faster automation development with AI, delivering nine times ROI through personalized process optimization. Our HR function operates at about half of the expected operating expense. We've automated 70% of HR operations with personalization at scale, equivalent to 15 full-time employees.[28] And this happened without any reduction in the HR workforce.

■　■　■

Customer personalization and career personalization are not separate revolutions. They are two expressions of the same shift: systems designed to sense variation and respond intelligently at scale.

This is the future: AI agents as both customer advocates and career partners that know your strengths, interests, and energy patterns. They proactively suggest experiences, solutions, opportunities, learning paths, and connections.

The opportunity directly connects to our twin-engine problem. The population engine can't be restarted – fewer workers are coming, period. But the productivity engine? That can be supercharged through more personalized work. When every person operates in their zone of genius, when AI handles what doesn't require human judgment, and when work shapes itself around individual strengths instead of forcing individuals into predetermined boxes, productivity doesn't increase by 10% or 20%. It multiplies exponentially.

Personalization is a critical ingredient to the future of the economy for consumers and workers alike. In The Five-Year Century, it's true that one size fits none.

10

The Trust Economy

Why Trust Is the Ultimate Competitive Advantage

In the 1760s, John Woolman made his living as a quiet, unremarkable merchant known for diligently keeping accounts, recording debts, and documenting transactions for others.

Woolman was meticulous and widely trusted. His ledgers were known to be accurate. His word rarely questioned. Yet as he reviewed contracts and bills of sale, he became increasingly troubled by what he was being asked to legitimize. Many of the transactions involved enslaved people. Merchants dismissed his concerns. *"It's just paperwork,"* they told him.

Woolman disagreed – and did something that defied economic logic at the time. He began refusing work.

When asked to write documents involving slavery, he declined calmly and without accusation. He accepted fewer clients. He earned less money. Through slow and often uncomfortable travel, he would go speak directly with other Quakers about what trust in commerce actually meant.[1]

Instead of being pushed out of business, Woolman's reputation strengthened. Transactions he documented carried unusual credibility. Disputes resolved faster. Credit extended more easily. His refusal to compromise reduced friction rather than creating it.[2]

Within Quaker commercial networks, this pattern repeated. Trust was not enforced through contracts or surveillance, but through transparency, consistency, and shared accountability. Reputation became infrastructure. Trust became an economic accelerant.

Today, we face a similar question, only the ledgers have been replaced by algorithms. Modern organizations increasingly rely on AI systems to make recommendations, allocate resources, and shape human outcomes. And just like Woolman's paperwork, these systems are often treated as neutral tools rather than moral artifacts.

But AI is never neutral. It reflects the data it is trained on, the assumptions embedded in its design, and the values of those who deploy it. When organizations outsource decision-making to models trained elsewhere – on data drawn from a narrow set of geographies, cultures, or socioeconomic groups – they risk scaling bias while believing they are scaling efficiency. In the age of AI, trust begins with authorship. Who defines the rules, whose realities are reflected, and who bears responsibility for the consequences.

◾ ◾ ◾

What is the value of trust today? Doesn't it feel like it's more valuable, but perhaps harder to achieve, than ever? Or was it always this valuable and hard to achieve, and are we only now realizing what it takes to earn, sustain, and protect it?

Think about the era of personalization at scale covered in the previous chapter. It cannot succeed without trust. From the outset, it's important to be precise about what kind of trust we're talking about. In the age of AI, trust has two equally critical dimensions. One is external: trust from customers, patients, and the public that the company or brand is serving them rather than exploiting them. The other is internal: trust from employees that the organization is a place where they can build a career, grow safely, and work alongside AI without being diminished.

To understand why internal trust has become a competitive advantage, consider what happens when trust erodes inside the organization in ways that could impact its ability to deliver externally.

Let's look at a national, publicly funded healthcare system in the United Kingdom, which operates as a federated network of regional trusts providing hospital, community, and healthcare services.

A director of people operations working at the UK healthcare system watched her recruitment team become overwhelmed by a crisis that threatened the foundation of British healthcare. With over 100,000 vacancies across the system and nearly two million job applications flowing through annually, her team was processing paperwork instead of building the workforce that would save lives.[3]

The problem had no end in sight. Each position took 8–12 weeks to fill. While candidates waited for responses, the best ones found other jobs. The ones who stayed often couldn't afford to wait any longer. Meanwhile, the director's recruitment team was burning out, creating a vicious cycle in which the people hired to solve the staffing crisis were becoming casualties of it.

Here's the question that changed everything for the UK healthcare system: What if the problem wasn't the people or even the process, but the fundamental relationship between humans and work?

■   ■   ■

On August 20, 2001, Enron's CEO sold 93,000 shares of his company's stock for roughly $2 million. That same day, he sent an email to all 21,000 Enron employees urging them to buy company shares. The stock was undervalued; he assured them. The company was on solid footing.[4]

Three and a half months later, Enron filed the largest corporate bankruptcy in American history. The stock the CEO quietly exited at over $20 per share traded for 26 cents. While senior executives protected their own wealth, Enron's 401(k) plan was in lockdown, preventing employees from selling as the stock plummeted. As a result, 15,000 employees' pension plans, holding $2.1 billion in assets, became essentially worthless. Trust was not merely broken but was consciously exploited.[5]

Enron didn't just destroy trust with investors and the public; it obliterated internal trust with its own employees. This dual collapse – internal and external – is the blueprint for how trust failure compounds at scale. But it wasn't an aberration. It was not simply the failure of abstract systems over time, but the predictable outcome of leaders who abused asymmetric information, authority, and power. It was the logical conclusion of a system that had been operating on a basis of mistrust for decades and enabled executives to act without accountability.

Looking further back, organizations in the Industrial Age spent decades perfecting systems of control while expecting loyalty in return. They tracked time to the minute while simultaneously asking employees to "go above and beyond" for the company mission. They demanded customer trust through glossy marketing campaigns while hiding fees in fine print and burying complaints in bureaucracy.

When the Information Age arrived, many companies simply digitized this experience rather than questioning it. They added software instead of stopwatches. They created compliance departments instead of building cultures of integrity. They confused monitoring with managing, and control with leadership.

Rather than using information-sharing systems to build employee trust, organizations expected compliance. Many still do. Externally, customers were expected to trust that their data was safe while companies sold it to the highest bidder. The reciprocal nature of trust was not prioritized.

That should have never worked – and it especially doesn't work today.

■ ■ ■

The 2026 Edelman Trust Barometer underscores how pervasive and consequential the trust deficit has become. Its findings show that seven in ten people worldwide are now hesitant or unwilling to trust someone who holds different values, beliefs, or perspectives, illustrating a retreat into insularity rather than trust across differences. On top of this, optimism about the future has collapsed: only about 32% of global respondents believe the next generation will be better off than the current one.[6]

Skepticism about leadership is high, as many respondents question whether CEOs and institutions are telling the full truth on issues that matter, including economic opportunity and the impact of technology.

Distrust of technology's benefits is also linked to economic concerns: according to the same research, 54% of low-income respondents believe generative AI will leave them behind rather than help them, and 44% of middle-income respondents feel the same, highlighting how AI fears intersect with trust and inequality.

This erosion of trust doesn't stop at the customer or external-facing boundary. Employees may carry the same skepticism into the workplace, particularly when AI and opaque decision-making are introduced without clarity or clear direction.

For leaders who must transform their teams within the confines of The Five-Year Century, this is why trust isn't just one KPI to track – it's the one currency that truly matters.

■ ■ ■

While trust shapes customer loyalty externally, its most immediate economic impact occurs internally – inside teams, workflows, and daily decisions about effort, creativity, and retention.

Can you measure trust the same way you measure revenue? Can you manage it the same way you manage inventory? Can you build it systematically rather than hope it emerges from good intentions?

Paul Zak, a neuroeconomist (yes, that's a real job), proved that you can. He discovered that trust has a biological marker, oxytocin. The same hormone that makes you bond with your baby also makes you a better employee. When Zak measured oxytocin levels in employees, he found something remarkable. Employees at high-trust companies are 50% more productive, 76% more engaged, 74% less stressed, and take 13% fewer sick days.[7] These boosts are bigger than any technology upgrade, any process improvement, any reorganization. And it comes from a hormone your brain produces for free when the conditions are right.

Luckily for us, Zak identified eight specific management behaviors that stimulate oxytocin production. The framework should be easy to remember, because it spells OXYTOCIN.

Ovation: This means publicly recognizing excellence. Not a $10 Starbucks gift card for a good job, but immediate, peer-driven, unexpected recognition. This alone accounts for about 2/3 of the variance in organizational trust.

Expectation: Set challenging but achievable goals. Any fan of John Doerr's *Measure What Matters* knows what we're talking about here: unambiguous objectives and key results (OKRs).

These induce "challenge stress," which is different from distress. Clear project-based goals with weekly milestones work best, provided they are communicated with clarity.

Yield: Give people space and discretion in how they do their work. This demonstrates trust from supervisors and increases ownership over outcomes. Not all leadership has to be hands-on.

Transfer: People focus their energies on what they care about most. Leaders can build trust by enabling job crafting. This means letting colleagues choose projects they care about and enabling them to work across functions. This might be one of the hardest actions for leaders to take, as it is completely counter to Industrial Age thinking.

Openness: This is synonymous with transparency and the broad sharing of information. Across industries, less than half of employees know their company's goals and strategies. Trust requires context and clarity.

Caring: To build trust, leaders must intentionally build relationships. And remember, Gen Z workers are incredibly good at sensing inauthenticity.

Invest: If people are not growing as human beings, their performance will suffer. Leaders must accept responsibility for facilitating whole-person growth, both professionally and personally.

Natural: When trust is modeled by those in charge, others follow. So, naturally, leaders must show vulnerability. This doesn't mean speaking one's mind in all situations but empathizing with the daily challenges that teams face in their pursuit of winning at business.[8]

This set of behaviors matters exponentially more in The Five-Year Century because they directly address our twin-engine problem. When oxytocin levels rise, productivity rises with them. Zak's research shows that high-trust employees are 50% more productive. That's not 50% better performance on the margins. That's nearly enough of an increase to achieve the 40% improvement we need to maintain economic output as the workforce declines.

The Industrial Age approach – relying on longer hours, intense monitoring, and increased pressure – is proving detrimental. In contrast, trust-based methods unleash discretionary effort, inspiring people to work harder, smarter, and more creatively when they trust their organization.

Patagonia offers one of the clearest demonstrations of how trust can compound externally. Consider one of the brand's most renowned marketing campaigns.

In 2011, they took out a full-page ad in *The New York Times* with a picture of their best-selling jacket and the headline, "Don't Buy This Jacket."[9] Marketing textbooks spontaneously combusted. Business schools called it insanity.

Patagonia's sales increased 30% that year.

Why? Because when you tell customers you care more about the planet than profits, and then actually act like it, something magical happens. They believe you. Patagonia's customer lifetime value is nine times the industry average. Their brand loyalty rate hit 98% compared to 13% for apparel overall.[10] They told people to buy less, and people responded by buying more.

Patagonia shows how companies can build trust with customers, but how about a company that builds trust with employees?

Costco demonstrates the internal mirror image of the same principle: when employees trust the organization, customers feel it without being marketed to.

Costco pays an average hourly wage of $24–26, versus $15 for the industry. Semi-annual bonuses average $4,000 for employees. The company covers 87% of health benefits, while competitors average 50%. It's no wonder most Costco workers have more than five years of tenure.[11]

As founder Jim Sinegal said, "When you take care of employees, they take care of customers."[12]

The pattern is consistent across industries. The Great Place to Work Institute analyzed over 100 million employee surveys over 30 years. High-trust companies delivered cumulative returns of 3,174% versus 907% for the Russell 1000. As of 2025, the outperformance continues, with trust-certified companies beating the market by a factor of 3.5.[13]

Trust, it would seem, literally prints money.

■ ■ ■

Remember our story about the UK healthcare system? They discovered something that changes everything about trust in the era of human-AI collaboration.

When the UK healthcare system introduced what they called "flobots" – AI assistants with actual names and staff profiles – something unexpected happened. Instead of fearing replacement, the human staff embraced them as teammates. Why? Because the leadership was radically transparent about the purpose: not to replace humans but to free them from soul-crushing administrative work so they could focus on what humans do best – care, create, and connect.[14]

The AI didn't hide behind corporate speak or pretend to be human. Each flobot had a name, a profile, and a clear role. They were introduced as team members, not replacement tools. The humans knew exactly what the flobots did, how they worked, and most importantly, how they made human work more meaningful, not less necessary.

The outcomes were impactful. The time to recruit new human team members dropped from eight weeks to six. Time to hire fell from twelve weeks to ten. And employee satisfaction soared. Freed from mindless paperwork, the recruitment team could focus on diversity initiatives, candidate experience, and strategic workforce planning. They went from processing papers to building the future of healthcare.[15]

Doing Good Is Doing Great

For the next generation, trust is evaluated holistically. Employees no longer separate how a company treats them internally from how it behaves externally. The latest generation entering the workforce doesn't just want to trust their employer. They want to trust that their employer is doing good out in the world.

Gen Z, the first digitally native generation, sees trust as a non-negotiable. 86% view purpose-driven work as essential. 75% of Gen Z prospects research company values before applying. They're incredibly adept at sensing inauthenticity, and they're not buying what most organizations are selling. They grew up swimming in a sea of corporate marketing, and they can smell performative goodness from miles away. CSR reports that read like PR campaigns actively raise their eyebrows. For this generation, trust isn't built through slogans or one-off donations. That expectation fundamentally changes how organizations must think about social impact and partnerships.

This distinction between symbolic giving and shared accountability is where many companies fall short. Just throwing money and technology tools at nonprofits rarely works because they need help implementing those tools. And when a company only donates (money, tech tools, software licenses, etc.), it could come across like a PR stunt. You have to back up the good you're doing, otherwise you erode trust with your workforce and the outside world. And if there's no measurable impact, no trust gets built.

Automation Anywhere co-founder and Chief Impact Officer Neeti Mehta Shukla says it clearly, "The idea is to partner with nonprofits that put the extra effort behind being human. If they do better, we all do better."

So, the key to more impactful social good is to partner closely with nonprofits and work alongside them to implement technology, rather than just handing it over. It means training staff to use and maintain AI and automation platforms and being on call when they have questions or need advice.

That philosophy becomes tangible when you look at what real partnership looks like in practice. Automation Anywhere partners closely with an NGO in India that operates on a mission that sounds almost impossibly ambitious: "No child in India should be deprived of education because of hunger." The NGO currently serves 2.35 million meals daily across 25,000 schools, aiming to reach five million meals by 2030. For many of these children, as the organization's CIO notes, "It's only one meal a day."

When Automation Anywhere partnered with the NGO, they worked together to implement a landmark collaboration to revolutionize charity operations in India. Rather than handing over tools and walking away, the two organizations co-designed solutions. With the support of AI, we partnered to transform key operational areas, including donor management, route optimization, and supply chain workflows to achieve greater efficiency, transparency, and scalability. Through the partnership, donor engagement processes were streamlined by up to 70%, with turnaround times dropping from over 20 hours to just 40 minutes. AI-backed automation greatly accelerates the NGO's mission to provide mid-day meals to five million children every school day and helps the organization focus more on strategic outreach and relationship-building efforts. The results are measurable, specific and undeniably real around how AI is doing good.

And the NGO didn't replace workers with agents. They redeployed workers in expansion efforts as they grew from 77 kitchens to 120. Some employees were trained and certified on the automation tools themselves and now support the agents that work alongside them.

When Mehta Shukla says, "Every rupee goes further, every meal reaches faster, every child is nourished better," that's not marketing copy, it's fact.[3] And when employees can point to 2.35 million children fed daily and know their work matters, that builds the kind of trust no marketing slogan can match.

The urgency of this work cannot be overstated. Just as AI transformation has accelerated across the enterprise to deliver positive impact, unfortunately there will continue to be global challenges like hunger or refugee displacement that need solving. For example, the number of global refugees globally has exploded due to wars, climate displacement, and internal conflicts. As of the latest United Nations High Commissioner for Refugees (UNHCR) global trends data, over 120 million people worldwide are forcibly displaced due to war, violence, persecution, and human rights violations – the highest number in history and roughly double the total from a decade ago.

It takes partnership to chip away at the biggest societal problems like this. As one small example, Automation Anywhere worked with a refugee-led cooperative that focuses on digital inclusion and job creation opportunities for the displaced. The partnership put AI to work with the launch of a Global Gateway Program that empowers refugees with digital skills and ultimately expands job inclusion opportunities for their digital career development.

According to the founder of the refugee-led cooperative, "Through our ecosystem for digital impact sourcing and Automation Anywhere's accessible product portfolio, we're providing career opportunities for refugees, regardless of their background, to contribute to the digital economy."

Investing in measurable solutions for global crises, rather than performative campaigns, builds trust that resonates with employees, customers, and communities. This is essential for meeting the shifting sands of The Five-Year Century. Gen Z understands companies must be profitable, but what matters to them is proof that purpose and profit can coexist, and that technology creates real good beyond financial returns.

Many decades ago, Nancy discovered the power of follow-through when working as the head of HR for Noah's New York Bagels. Noah's couldn't give out free bagels to everyone, and they didn't have any technology to deploy. So, instead they became great neighbors. Before new hires even learned the correct way to slice a bagel, their employer had them out in the community, painting older people's homes, planting trees in parks, and cleaning up local beaches. The result? People thought they were the best neighbor on Earth. Young people wanted to work for Noah's. Customers became almost cult-like in their loyalty. Trust, it turns out, accelerates.

Accelerating Trust in The Five-Year Century

The time compression of The Five-Year Century creates a problem for leaders needing to build trust at speed and scale. Trust historically takes years to build and seconds to destroy. Patagonia spent decades earning customer trust before the "Don't Buy This Jacket" campaign would work. Costco built its reputation over generations. The healthcare system referenced earlier has been one of the UK's most trusted institutions for 75 years. You might announce a partnership with a nonprofit, but it's going to take time to see the impact.

But what happens when you need to build trust in months, not decades?

The Five-Year Century creates a paradox. Trust matters more than ever because humans are scarce and each one is infinitely more valuable. But the timeline to build trust has collapsed along with everything else.

This compression creates an uncomfortable truth: we are all traversing the unknown. No organization, regulator, or technologist fully understands where AI will ultimately lead, and the pace of change far outstrips our historical ability to adapt. In such an environment, speed without governance is not progress, but drift.

Deploying AI without clear principles, accountability, and contextual awareness is like moving at machine speed without a rudder. Responsible leadership in the AI age does not mean waiting for certainty; it means deciding, in advance, how systems will be governed when certainty is unavailable. AI does not replace trust but amplifies whatever trust model already exists.

Traditional trust-building relied on repeated interactions over time. You proved trustworthy through consistent performance across years. In contrast, AI reshapes trust through frequency, visibility, and consistency of interaction. AI systems can autonomously create thousands of micro-interactions daily, each one building or destroying trust. An AI coach that remembers preferences, anticipates needs, and delivers value without judgment can build trust faster than a human manager who sees an employee once a week in a scheduled one-on-one.

The UK healthcare system didn't spend years building trust before deploying flobots. They treated trust as a design requirement, not an outcome. Trust was built through radical transparency from day one with clear communication about purpose, visible AI team members with names and roles, and immediate evidence that the technology made human work more meaningful. Trust accumulated through daily interactions, not annual initiatives.

The companies that win in The Five-Year Century understand that trust at speed requires different mechanisms. You can't wait for organic trust to emerge. You must intentionally design systems that create repeatable, positive trust moments at scale. That means generating consistent, low-friction interactions between humans and AI inside the organization, while simultaneously demonstrating measurable impact outside the organization.

Here's where AI becomes a practical trust accelerator. AI-powered coaching can provide continuous, judgment-free feedback. Unlike human leaders who may forget, postpone, or unconsciously favor some employees over others, AI systems are consistent by design. They remember context, detect patterns, and surface relevant guidance continuously. Used correctly, they reduce friction, not autonomy. With frequent touchpoints, employees often build trust with these systems faster than with senior leaders because the interaction is immediate, predictable, and safe. As a result, people ask AI questions they would never ask their boss.

So, here is a concrete initiative leaders can start immediately: identify and automate systems that reinforce positive behaviors – fairness, transparency, recognition, autonomy, and growth – while explicitly eliminating systems that undermine them. Use AI to increase clarity, consistency, and support, but not to monitor, score, or control.

The team at the UK healthcare system proved that even under overwhelming demand, scarce resources, and severe burnout, trust can still be rebuilt quickly when leaders treat it as an operating discipline. When humans trust the organization, trust the technology, and trust each other, execution accelerates and resilience follows.

The question isn't whether trust matters in the AI age. The question is whether leaders will design for it deliberately and fast enough to matter.

A Framework for Responsible AI

Today's leaders must recognize both the transformative power of AI and automation, along with the responsibility that comes with it. That's why Automation Anywhere, with the support of our customers and partners, is committed to building AI systems that not only comply with global regulations but uphold the highest ethical standards.

Responsible AI also requires sovereignty, or the ability for organizations and societies to shape how AI systems are trained, deployed, localized, and governed in alignment with their values and communities. When AI systems are designed to serve only a narrow demographic or economic reality, they do more than introduce bias; they erode trust at scale.

In a world where AI increasingly mediates opportunity, access, and judgment, organizations must take responsibility not only for what their systems can do, but for whom they work, whom they exclude, and whose realities they reflect.

Our Responsible AI Framework below can serve as the foundation of this commitment for your own efforts, shaping how to design, deploy, and govern AI to promote transparency, fairness, and accountability. We believe responsible AI requires proactive design, not reactive correction. To that end, our policies and practices align with seven core principles, as follows:

1. **Ethics:** We must be deeply committed to ethical AI development grounded in transparency, fairness, and human dignity. Systems must be designed to be governed by people, prevent harm, and respect human rights, freedom, and diversity.

2. **Security:** Security is embedded across the AI lifecycle – from design through deployment and maintenance. AI platforms must always provide safeguards against emerging threats and enable customers to establish their own responsible AI frameworks when using automation technologies.

3. **Privacy:** We must prioritize the protection of individual identity by providing clarity, control, and oversight over how data is stored, accessed, and used. Approaches must respect stakeholder intent and ensure data is handled only for its intended purposes.

4. **Reliability:** Trustworthy AI must be reliable. We must focus on building robust models, measuring accuracy and resilience, and transparently explaining outputs and actions. Continuous improvement and disciplined measurement are central to any top approach.

5. **Accessibility:** We must be committed to making AI inclusive and globally accessible. Products should support diverse users, languages, and cultures, complemented by training programs and scholarships that expand access to the jobs of the future.

6. **Transparency:** Transparency is essential to trust. We must communicate openly about products, policies, and AI decision-making, while prioritizing minimal and responsible data use.

7. **Accountability:** Human oversight remains essential. By involving people throughout the AI lifecycle, accountability is built into every stage of development and deployment.

Together, these principles reflect our belief that trust is not an aspiration – it is an operating discipline. And in the age of AI, it is the foundation on which sustainable progress is built.

11

The Skills Race No One Can Sit Out

The World Is Not Short on Talent – Only on Access

The skills race created by technology transformation is often discussed in abstract terms – millions of jobs displaced, millions more created, timelines accelerating faster than institutions can adapt. However, the reality of reskilling is not abstract. It is deeply human, deeply local, and unevenly distributed.

To understand what reskilling actually looks like when it succeeds and why learning can no longer be left to time, it helps to start far from corporate headquarters, product roadmaps, or executive strategy decks.

Let's look at the Mississippi Delta as one example. Specifically, Clarksdale, Mississippi, an area long challenged by depopulation, limited employment opportunities, and barriers to entry into high-growth sectors.

This is a region with deep cultural roots, resilience, and talent – one that has contributed enormously to American history, music, and community life, even as economic opportunity has not always kept pace with that potential.[1,2,3,4]

It's a place where you may hear young people saying things like:

"The only options for work are fast food, farming or being a truck driver."

"In my job as an overnight worker at a retail store, I work all night and then sleep all day, and don't have enough time to be with my son."

"I have always been interested in electronics and technology, but I never thought there would be any career opportunities for that in the state of Mississippi."

Unfortunately, these statements are not unique to any one place in America or around the world. Versions of them can be heard in rural communities, post-industrial cities, and underserved regions across the globe. Regardless of comparison, it's fair to say that the Mississippi Delta faces its share of economic challenges.

It's for this reason that Automation Anywhere partnered with a public benefit corporation focused on impact sourcing to support a program that reskilled members of the community in Clarksdale. The intent was not to "fix" a community, but to work alongside local leaders and residents to remove barriers that had little to do with ability and everything to do with access.

Through the initiative, local residents received paid foundation, technical, and process training in automation skills and were able to become certified automation developers in as little as six months. The program helped reskill hundreds of associates from across the region, bringing new careers and income security to an area that previously lacked access to tech pathways, and offering hundreds of high-value, tech-enabled job opportunities that made a tangible difference for participating individuals and their families. Many participants had the opportunity to move from minimum-wage jobs into careers where they manage automation deployments and support business transformation.

The types of things you could hear the same young people mentioning after the program says it all:

"I am now proficient in computer technology and I'm more business savvy. Every day, I think about what I can create. I have a career and the feeling that I am truly part of something great."

"I never saw myself as a leader or leading anyone. Now as an automation trainer, I still get little butterflies, but I love teaching others and learning together."

"I can finally do the things I love with my child because of this opportunity."

It's important to be clear about what this program is, and what it is not. It is not a silver bullet, nor does it define the future of the Mississippi Delta. It represents one small but meaningful intervention in people's lives. This model can be especially consequential in regions and communities where traditional educational pathways and degrees are scarce, expensive, or structurally out of reach. Whether it's underserved communities in the US, Africa, Nepal or anywhere, people can now acquire market-relevant skills through 4–12 weeks of applied learning, supported by AI-driven coaching, localized content, and real project work.

Of course, this is not a promise that AI will equalize outcomes on its own. But it is a realistic recognition that when learning accelerates and barriers fall, the global talent pool expands and the skills race becomes not just faster, but more inclusive.

■ ■ ■

Reskilling and Upskilling in the Age of AI

AI is creating two very different workforce transformation challenges at the same time. One is reskilling – creating entirely new pathways for people who have been structurally excluded from high-growth work or whose existing roles are disappearing. The other is upskilling – evolving the capabilities of people who are already employed inside organizations, but whose work is being reshaped by AI. A customer service representative who learns to manage AI-powered support systems is upskilling. A customer service representative who becomes a data analyst is reskilling.

Both are necessary. Both require investment. But they solve different problems for different populations.

Historically, upskilling happened through a combination of on-the-job learning and formal education. Workers learned by doing, failing, observing, and asking. A junior accountant processed hundreds of invoices, made small errors that a senior colleague caught, watched how partners navigated client conversations, and asked questions during the natural flow of work. Formal training and advanced degrees supplemented this experiential foundation, but they rarely replaced it. The most important judgment – such as knowing when the standard approach doesn't apply or sensing when something feels wrong before you can articulate why – came from accumulated experience, not coursework.

This model is breaking down. Across industries, the junior work that once served as a training ground is disappearing into AI systems. Law firms deploy AI that performs document review faster and more accurately than first-year associates. Engineering teams use AI coding assistants that handle the routine programming tasks that once built foundational skills. Financial services firms automate the analysis that junior analysts used to spend years mastering. The entry-level work is being done more and more by machines. And with it goes the learning laboratory that created the next generation of senior professionals.

If workers are learning less by hands-on doing, they need deliberate exposure to decision-making contexts. This requires intentional design, not hope. Organizations must create rotation programs that expose junior employees to multiple functions quickly rather than allowing them to specialize narrowly in one area that might disappear. They must pair junior workers with senior colleagues specifically to observe judgment calls, not just to assist with tasks. They must simulate the small failures that teach discernment, like creating safe environments where people can make mistakes and learn from them before the stakes get high.

This creates a gap that few organizations have confronted directly. As senior workers retire or leave the workforce, less organizations will have developed the judgment that comes from years of hands-on experience. The traditional pipeline assumed that today's junior employees would become tomorrow's senior experts through natural progression. But if the junior work gets transformed, so does the progression.

The solution requires rethinking what new hires need to learn. Technical skills remain important, but they're no longer sufficient alone – and they're increasingly perishable as AI capabilities expand. The durable capabilities are the ones that humans must continue to immerse themselves in: critical thinking that questions assumptions, business context that connects technical work to strategic outcomes, cross-stakeholder communication that navigates competing interests, and ethical reasoning that recognizes when efficiency conflicts with values. These have always mattered, but organizations could once assume employees would absorb them gradually through years of experience.

This is why upskilling in the Age of AI looks fundamentally different from upskilling in previous eras. It's not about adding technical certifications to existing experiential foundations. It's about deliberately constructing the experiential foundations that used to emerge organically, while simultaneously building capabilities that transcend any particular technical skill. The organizations that figure this out will develop talent that competitors cannot easily replicate. Those that don't will find themselves increasingly dependent on a shrinking pool of senior professionals whose expertise cannot be transferred because the transfer mechanisms have broken down.

The talent pipeline matters for a reason that connects directly to the productivity math of The Five-Year Century. If organizations need to reach $500,000 in value created per employee, then every new hire must reach that number quickly. A new employee who takes three years to become fully productive is a luxury that shrinking workforces cannot afford.

For companies to survive in The Five-Year Century, all employees need to contribute meaningful value faster than previous generations did. That requires organizations to invest in skills development infrastructure that compresses learning timelines – not by cutting corners, but by deliberately designing the exposure, feedback and capability-building that used to happen over years. The companies that master this will be able to grow without requiring proportional increases in headcount.

■ ■ ■

Traditional employment models often treat workers as fixed assets that are hired for specific skills, expected to perform those skills indefinitely and rise up the career ladder in their function. A transformation mindset requires continuous value creation on both sides. Companies must invest in developing their people; employees must embrace ongoing growth and cross-functional work that breaks down hierarchies between departments. Surviving and thriving in The Five-Year Century will require everyone to focus on skills development.

We cannot yet name most of the millions of new roles that AI will create. They don't exist yet and have not yet been imagined. We can project the displacement with reasonable accuracy because the work being automated follows patterns, repetitive tasks, rules-driven decisions, and process execution at scale.

This asymmetry echoes every major technological transformation in history. When Cyrus McCormick demonstrated his mechanical reaper in a Virginia field in 1831, the farmers watching couldn't have imagined automobile assembly lines, airline pilots or software engineers. The farm laborers displaced by mechanized agriculture couldn't have conceived of the manufacturing jobs, transportation networks, and service industries their grandchildren would occupy. McCormick's reaper didn't just eliminate jobs but made entirely new categories of human endeavor possible. AI will do the same to us, at a pace and scale that dwarfs everything that came before.

The potential net job gain is meaningless if displaced workers can't transition to new roles. Not every transition will be severely different, but to employees who have been doing one job their whole life, only to be told they need to upskill into another, it might feel impossible.

A healthy labor ecosystem requires companies to be net contributors to human capability, not just extractors of existing skills. The Industrial Age model treated workers as interchangeable inputs to be consumed – hire them with the skills they have, use those skills until they're depleted or obsolete, then replace them with fresh inputs. The Age of AI demands something fundamentally different. Organizations must develop capabilities that benefit the whole system, building human potential rather than simply burning through it.

This is also a competitive strategy. Organizations that build reputations as talent developers attract better candidates in the first place. They retain them longer because people stay where they're growing. They create alumni networks that become customers, partners and referral sources. The investment in skills development pays dividends across every dimension of organizational performance. And critically, it sustains the labor ecosystem that every company depends on. When organizations extract without developing, they're mining a finite resource. When they develop while extracting, they're cultivating a renewable one.

Thankfully, many of the top technology companies globally are banding together to recognize the heightened need for skills development. As announced at the World Economic Forum in Davos in January 2026, 25 of the world's leading global technology companies – including Automation Anywhere alongside Accenture, Salesforce, Cognizant, Snowflake, and more – have pledged to provide technology access, skills training, and career pathways to 120 million people globally. As part of this coalition, Automation Anywhere has specifically committed to support two million individuals through skills development programs aimed at preparing workers for roles in an AI and automation-driven economy. While this global technology pledge is only the beginning of a long journey ahead for us and the technology community, it's a step in the right direction to ensure we give workers – including those without formal academic credentials or technical backgrounds – a chance to equip themselves with the skills needed to thrive in The Five-Year Century.

■ ■ ■

While reskilling opens doors for those previously excluded, the other half of the skills race is unfolding inside organizations themselves. For employees already credentialed and contributing, the challenge is not access, but evolution.

What matters about this next story is not about Automation Anywhere itself, but the possibilities it reveals.

The controllership function within a finance department has historically been one of the most rules-bound parts of the enterprise. Its mandate is accuracy, compliance, and control, often achieved through layers of manual review, checklists, and signoffs designed to reduce risk. But this same structure has also made controllership brittle in the face of growing transaction complexity.

Few areas illustrate this better than revenue recognition.

Every company registered in the United States must comply with ASC 606, the accounting standard governing how revenue contracts are evaluated, interpreted, and recognized. The standard itself spans nearly 100,000 pages of guidance and interpretations. In practice, revenue accounting teams often distill this complexity into 30–40 checklist items that must be evaluated for every customer contract, often manually.

Each customer order form must be reviewed against these rules to determine:

- Performance obligations and evaluate if they are distinct
- How transaction value of the order form should be allocated to different performance obligations
- How revenue allocated to each performance obligation can be recognized
- What additional documentation, clarification or approvals are required

Traditionally, this work has been performed by highly trained accountants acting as human rule engines who read contracts, cross-reference guidance, and apply judgment under heavy workloads. The result is a function that is critical, but often slow and difficult to scale.

As part of Automation Anywhere's AI-first transformation journey, the controller organization fed their interpretative guidance on the most applicable sections of the ASC 606-guide into an AI-powered "Rev Rec Agent" capable of evaluating contracts against the full body of rules and principles. The agent can assess each contract, determine which rules apply, identify required actions, and route exceptions for human review when judgment truly matters.

The results were immediate:

- Processing time improved by 2–3×
- Productivity reached 10–12 contracts per hour, per agent
- Operational efficiency increased by 140%
- Cost efficiency improved by approximately 85%

What makes this example transformative is not just the efficiency gain, but the redefinition of the controller role through AI upskilling. As revenue recognition is only one of dozens of rule-intensive processes inside a typical controller organization, Automation Anywhere's controller, Shantha Krishnaswamy, says the possibilities are endless.

"Our vision is to create a fully autonomous controllership that acts as a CFO assistant for all things financial intelligence. We are confident we will get there."

■ ■ ■

Designing Work for What Humans Do Best

If upskilling is the central challenge for the AI-first enterprise, then the next question becomes unavoidable: Where should we focus?

The work that AI cannot do as well as us is precisely the work that creates the most value: judgment, context, relationships and ethics. These capabilities have always mattered, but they have often been overshadowed by the technical skills that dominate job descriptions and hiring criteria. In The Five-Year Century, the balance flips. Part of the technical execution becomes table stakes: it's something AI provides abundantly. Human value concentrates in the capabilities that remain stubbornly, irreducibly human.

Critical thinking and judgment sit at the top of this list. AI systems excel at pattern recognition but struggle to assess whether their outputs make sense in context. An LLM can generate a contract clause that is grammatically perfect and legally plausible but entirely wrong for the specific situation. A forecasting algorithm can extrapolate trends with mathematical precision while missing the obvious fact that market conditions have fundamentally changed. Humans must evaluate AI outputs for reasonableness, know when to override recommendations, and understand the limitations of pattern-based systems. This isn't about distrusting AI, but about using it intelligently.

Business context is equally critical. A junior employee who only knows how to process invoices adds limited value. One who understands how invoice processing connects to cash flow, vendor relationships, and financial reporting can identify problems that the process itself doesn't capture. They can recognize when rules should be broken and when the standard approach will produce a technically correct but strategically wrong outcome. This contextual understanding is what transforms task execution into business contribution.

Cross-stakeholder communication represents another irreplaceable human capability. AI can generate text, but it cannot build meaningful relationships that cut across departments. It can summarize technical findings, but it cannot read the room when presenting them to skeptical executives. Organizations run on informal influence as much as formal authority – knowing who to talk to, how to frame requests, when to push, and when to wait. As AI increases transparency into workflows, decisions, and trade-offs, some of the operational politics tied to information asymmetry and hidden work begins to fall away – what remains is not maneuvering for control, but human judgment about priorities, trade-offs, and consequences. These skills require emotional intelligence, awareness and the kind of trust that only accumulates through repeated human interaction.

Ethical reasoning is one of the most important capabilities of all. AI systems optimize for the objectives they're given, but they don't question whether those objectives are right. They can't recognize when efficiency creates injustice, when a technically optimal solution harms vulnerable stakeholders, or when following the rules violates their spirit. Humans must identify when AI recommendations create ethical problems, understand whose interests are served by different decisions, and take responsibility for outcomes rather than hiding behind processes. "The algorithm decided" is not an acceptable answer when the decision causes harm.

In an outcome-oriented organization, these four capabilities – critical thinking, business context, cross-stakeholder communication, and ethical reasoning – are not abstract traits, but are the basis of ownership where humans remain accountable for results even as work is executed by a combination of people and AI agents.

Since AI-first enterprises are fundamentally oriented around outcomes rather than activities, we must design roles so people spend their time where judgment and learning matter most. This shift shows up clearly in how junior work is reimagined.

The first strategy positions junior workers as AI supervisors rather than AI replacements. Take invoice processing, for example. The outcome is no longer throughput alone, but accuracy, resilience, and faster human learning at scale. Instead of processing invoices, junior employees review AI-processed invoices, catch errors and handle exceptions. This actually accelerates learning. Rather than processing 100 invoices to find one anomaly, they see every anomaly AI flags across 10,000 invoices. They encounter in a week the variety that would have taken months to experience under the old model. More importantly, they learn the reasons behind rules, not just the rules themselves.

When you ask a junior employee to evaluate whether AI correctly flagged an exception, they must understand the underlying logic – why this pattern matters, what it might indicate and what the consequences of missing it would be. A junior analyst reviewing AI-generated forecasts learns what makes a forecast reasonable or suspicious faster than they would when building forecasts manually, because they see more forecasts and focus on evaluation rather than calculation.

The second strategy transforms passive observation into active learning through shadow programs with explicit debriefs. Junior workers have historically observed senior workers, but observation alone transfers little knowledge. The critical addition is structured debriefing conversations in which senior workers explain their reasoning. "I noticed you paused when the client said X. What were you thinking?" "Why did you decide to push back on that request instead of accommodating it?" "What signals told you this deal was going sideways?" These conversations make tacit knowledge explicit. Senior professionals often can't articulate what they know until someone asks the right questions. The debrief structure forces that articulation, converting decades of accumulated judgment into transferable insight.

The third strategy embraces rapid rotation rather than deep specialization. Traditional career development often kept workers in narrow functional silos for years, building deep expertise in one area before moving to another. In an AI world, T-shaped skills matter more – broad understanding across functions with depth in one or two areas they are especially talented in or passionate about. Rotation programs that expose junior workers to multiple functions quickly build the cross-functional understanding that AI lacks. An employee who has worked in sales, marketing, operations, and finance understands how decisions in one area ripple through the others. They can spot problems that siloed, function-driven specialists miss. They can communicate across organizational boundaries because they've lived on both sides. This breadth becomes increasingly valuable as AI handles the routine work within each function, leaving humans to manage the connections between them.

The fourth strategy involves deliberate failure design. Learning requires making mistakes, but modern organizations often protect junior employees from consequences, either by limiting their decision authority or by catching errors before they matter. This protection, well-intentioned as it is, prevents the calibration that comes from experiencing the results of your own judgment. Organizations need low-stakes environments where junior workers make decisions with AI support and experience real consequences. Simulations can recreate high-pressure scenarios without actual risk. Sandboxed projects can give junior employees ownership of outcomes that matter but won't sink the company if they go wrong. Managed client accounts can provide real responsibility with appropriate guardrails. The goal isn't to punish failure but to create the feedback loops that teach judgment before the stakes get high.

These four strategies share a common thread; they replace the incidental learning that used to occur through routine work with intentional learning designed for a world in which routine work can be potentially automated. Junior employees as AI supervisors. Shadow programs with structured debriefs. Rapid functional rotation. Deliberate failure design. None of these is revolutionary in concept, but few organizations have implemented them systematically for the age of AI.

The organizations that implement these strategies will build capabilities that competitors cannot easily replicate. Talent development becomes a competitive moat. The companies that figure out how to accelerate human judgment in an AI-augmented environment will have workforces that are genuinely differentiated – not because they have better AI, but because they have humans who know how to use AI wisely. That combination of technological capability and human judgment is what creates durable advantage.

■ ■ ■

The implicit promise of Industrial Age employment was simple: *here is your job, learn it, do it well, and over time you will advance.* Workers invested years mastering stable skills. Employers reinforced that stability through fixed job descriptions, linear promotion paths, and performance systems optimized for repetition and efficiency. The entire model assumed that work itself would remain largely unchanged.

That promise is no longer true, and pretending otherwise does new hires a disservice.

The more honest promise in the Age of AI must be explicit from day one: *This is your starting point, not your destination.* The work will change. Your tools will change. The value you create will change. The organization's responsibility is to help you evolve fast enough to stay valuable – here and anywhere else your career takes you. This is not a threat; it is a more transparent and resilient foundation for the employment relationship.

Organizations that adopt this framing prepare people for transformation instead of shocking them with it later. They introduce AI tools immediately – not as replacements, but as developmental partners. They make learning visible inside the flow of work rather than isolating it in periodic training programs. Skill development stops being remedial and becomes a shared expectation of modern work.

This shift also changes how careers are described. Instead of five-year plans built around static roles, new hires build portfolios of capabilities that travel across functions. Instead of measuring progress by tenure, organizations measure growth in judgment, context, and contribution. Learning is no longer something that happens before work begins or after hours – it becomes inseparable from the work itself. The message is clear: *Your value depends on your ability to keep developing, and we are investing in that development because it benefits both of us.*

Redeployment requires an equally important reframing. In the Industrial Age, redeployment was treated as a consolation prize – an admission that something had gone wrong. The language implied failure, charity, or decline, even when pay and responsibility remained intact. Workers absorbed that stigma, and trust eroded accordingly.

In the Age of AI, redeployment must be understood differently. The work is evolving, so the contribution must evolve with it. Framed correctly, redeployment becomes a signal of progress rather than loss – a deliberate redesign of how a person's capabilities are applied as the organization changes. It invites participation instead of compliance and reinforces the idea that the organization values the human being, not just the role they once occupied.

But this framing only works if it is backed by action. When employees see colleagues move from automated or shrinking roles into meaningful new work – with real investment and real respect – change becomes less frightening and more navigable. When redeployment feels like abandonment, no amount of messaging can restore trust.

This is where organizational values are revealed. It is easy to celebrate people when times are good. The real test comes when AI reshapes the work someone has done for years. Not every role will translate cleanly, and not every person will be able to make the transition. Those limits are real. What matters is how leaders respond to their employees. Do they diminish those whose roles are changing, or invest in developing them? Not every transition for every employee will succeed, but choosing to make a disciplined attempt reveals what leaders truly believe about their people.

The organizations that thrive in The Five-Year Century will treat human capability development as a core strategic function, not an HR initiative. Upskilling cannot sit at the margins, funded only after other priorities are met. It must be resourced and measured with the same rigor as product development, infrastructure, or market expansion.

With population growth slowing and productivity demands accelerating, the math is unforgiving. Every new hire must contribute meaningful value faster than previous generations did. That speed cannot be achieved by squeezing people harder – it requires deliberately designed learning, faster exposure to judgment-rich work, and continuous capability building alongside AI.

Whether someone begins their journey in a community like Clarksdale, Mississippi, or inside a global enterprise, the underlying question is the same: *How quickly can human capability evolve alongside machines?* The starting points differ. The contexts differ. But the future of work depends on how intentionally organizations invest in the people doing the work.

So, the defining question is not *what can AI do?*

Instead, *why should this be human work?*

Once that question is asked honestly, it becomes clear that much of what we call knowledge work is already AI-ready – still performed by people only because organizational models have not yet caught up. The opportunity ahead is not to diminish human contribution, but to elevate it.

If organizations help employees understand upskilling and redeployment as pathways to more meaningful work – rather than signals of obsolescence – people can focus their energy where it matters most: judgment, context, relationships, and ethics. Surrounded by millions of AI agents, humans will do the work that only humans can do – and finally do it at their full potential.

Work Worthy of Human Potential

AT THE CUSP of The Five-Year Century, we face a pivotal choice: Will we use AI to bend people to machines or design technology to serve human needs? That is our choice.

For nearly two centuries, economies flew on twin engines: population growth supplying more workers and productivity growth extracting more value from each one. That model is ending. The population engine hasn't stalled; it's reversing. Productivity growth has flatlined, despite trillions invested in digital transformation. The plane is losing altitude.

But here's what gives us hope: Every constraint and illusion we've described is also a wide-eyed opportunity. The demographic shift threatening economic stability also creates a chance for work to become human again. For too long, we've asked people to do tasks that didn't require their humanity – repetitive processes, mundane routines, and soul-crushing work machines originally couldn't handle. We trained Lucy Larcom and her descendants to work by the bell, submit to mechanical time and become system extensions, not authors of their contributions. We built management philosophies assuming humans were unreliable without supervision. We designed organizations that treated workers as interchangeable parts, to the detriment of employees, customers, and communities.

This book began with an unlikely partnership – a Chicago-native CHRO who problem-solves with humor and a software engineer turned CEO from India who envisions human potential unleashed by technology. We see the world differently in many ways. Yet we share a deep conviction: Humans are meant for more. The systems we've inherited over the centuries aren't the best we can build. The world's breakthrough technologies like AI offer a chance to finally get it right.

For too long, we've reduced people to functions and job titles rather than recognizing that an HR leader may also be a technologist building robots on weekends or a finance professional may possess deep creative intuition. Countless forms of human capability remain invisible simply because our organizations were never designed to see beyond roles and titles. Often our team members are more than the roles they perform. It is time we find a way to tap into all of their strengths.

This is undoubtedly the biggest opportunity yet to change this. We know the math demands action. We know the technology exists to drive exponential change. It will take bold leadership to drive accelerated outcomes in the age of AI.

It's time to step forward and build the future we all deserve.

Acknowledgments

It is tempting to acknowledge every person I have ever met. However, the people who have most helped me foment my thinking about The Five-Year Century and deserve my eternal gratitude are:

Bill Raduchel, my friend, mentor, and tormentor, who makes me think harder, argue better, and use language with precision. Forrest Whyte, my crazy-smart partner in the crime of pushing boundaries. Danny Speros, thoughtful and wise, who always has a point of view that inspires me. Vince Han, the powerful voice of young CEOs whose view of this work changed my view of this work. Cathy and Phil Dixon, whose encouragement filled the tank when energy and inspiration ran low. Paul Fruin, whose patience, talent, and sharp editorial eye helped two very different authors bring about one cohesive book. Mihir Shukla, my friend, colleague, and co-author for asking the most infuriating and thought-provoking questions of my career. What a privilege it is to share this with Mihir.

To Drew and Charlotte, go create the future your YaYa can only dream of.

Finally, to Kem Hauge, who married a girl who said she was going to write a book. . .he waited 51 years to see it and never gave up on that girl.

Nancy

■ ■ ■

To Automation Anywhere, my teammates, our amazing customers, and partners – almost everything in this book is a result of us learning together and dreaming up what the world could be and not just what it is.

To my fellow co-founders, Neeti, Ankur, and Rushabh, for believing in our crazy idea before anyone else did and sticking to it.

To Nancy, my co-author, for always listening to my unconventional ideas, elevating them with her wisdom and experience, and bringing them to life. To Paul Fruin, whose patience and precision shaped these pages.

To my kids, who keep reminding me every day that the disruption of one generation is common sense for the next.

To my dad, a journalist – everything you ever read to me has quietly led to this moment.

To my wonderful family, from whom I continue to learn about life, values, love, and in a world where you can do many things, doing what is worth doing. To my mom and Neeti for being my rock – encouraging, always present.

Mihir

Authors' Biographies

Mihir Shukla is the Chairman, CEO, and co-founder of Automation Anywhere, a global leader in AI and agentic automation. A technologist, entrepreneur, and futurist, he is a lifelong student of how work gets done – studying as much from the history of the Industrial Age as from the frontiers of artificial intelligence. He views the future of work not as a technological problem to be solved, but as a leadership challenge – one that requires designing systems where people can learn, adapt, and thrive alongside intelligent machines. For Mihir, technology sets the possibilities, but it is leaders who ultimately determine the outcomes.

Mihir's career has spanned multiple multi-billion-dollar journeys at the forefront of technology revolutions, such as the internet, search, cloud computing, e-commerce, and smartphones. Through these transformations, he has helped shape new software categories to reimagine how people and machines work together.

Mihir co-founded Automation Anywhere in 2003 and has led the company through various milestones during its rapid growth journey, including pioneering multiple technology breakthroughs and building an award-winning culture.

A recognized tech visionary, Mihir is a frequent voice in global conversations on automation, AI, and workforce transformation, advising business leaders and institutions on how to build resilient, inclusive systems of work in an era of rapid change. In this book, Mihir brings together historical perspective, practical insight, and future-oriented thinking shaped by a deep belief in leadership as a human responsibility.

Mihir is married to his co-founder, Neeti Mehta Shukla, and they have three daughters.

■   ■   ■

Nancy Hauge is a veteran human resources leader whose 40-year career has spanned some of the most dynamic companies in Silicon Valley and beyond. Beginning her career with aspirations in comedy and the arts, Nancy brings an improvisational mindset to her career, viewing people as the most compelling and unpredictable part of business. A native Chicagoan who has worked globally, she is known for candid insight, wit, and an insistence that organizations can be both high-performing and deeply human.

Nancy has been recognized by *HRO Today* as "CHRO of the Year" through her relentless focus on innovation. Additional recognition includes being named by *HR Leadership* as one of the "Top 100 HR Tech Influencers" and by *Silicon Valley Business Journal* as one of the "100 Women of Influence" in Silicon Valley.

She has served on numerous leadership boards in her career across industries, including with Wilmington Pharmaceuticals, Magnus Health, Regroup, Holy Names College, and the Cameron School of Business at the University of North Carolina at Wilmington.

Nancy has been married to the award-winning composer, Kem Hauge, for over 50 years.

Notes

Chapter 1

1. Osterman, Michelle J. K., Brady E. Hamilton, Joyce A. Martin, Anne K. Driscoll, and Claudia P. Valenzuela. Births: Final Data for 2023. *National Vital Statistics Reports* 74, no. 1 (March 18, 2025). Hyattsville, MD: National Center for Health Statistics. https://doi.org/10.15620/cdc/175204
2. "Italy - Fertility Rate, Total (Births per Woman)." 2025. *Trading Economics*, October. https://tradingeconomics.com/italy/fertility-rate-total-births-per-woman-wb-data.html
3. Ibid.
4. United Nations, Department of Economic and Social Affairs, Population Division, *World Population Prospects 2024: Summary of Results* (New York: United Nations, July 2024), https://population.un.org/wpp/assets/Files/WPP2024_Summary-of-Results.pdf
5. Congressional Budget Office, *The Demographic Outlook: 2025 to 2055* (Washington, DC: Congressional Budget Office, January 2025), https://www.cbo.gov/publication/61164
6. Persol Research and Consulting Co. and Chuo University Institute of Economic Research, *Labor Market Future Forecasts 2035* (Tokyo: Persol Research and Consulting, October 2024), https://www.chuo-u.ac.jp/english/news/2024/11/77298/

7. Enghin Atalay, Sebastian Sotelo, and Daniel Tannenbaum, "The Mysterious Slowdown in U.S. Manufacturing Productivity," *Liberty Street Economics* (blog), Federal Reserve Bank of New York, July 11, 2024, revised November 12, 2024, https://libertystreeteconomics.newyorkfed.org/2024/07/the-mysterious-slowdown-in-u-s-manufacturing-productivity/

8. Federal Reserve Bank of Chicago. Economic Perspectives, Volume 49, Number 1 (2025): "*Why U.S. Productivity Growth Has Been So Slow and Uneven.*" (Chicago, IL: Federal Reserve Bank of Chicago, 2025), https://www.chicagofed.org/publications/economic-perspectives/2025/1

9. Organisation for Economic Co-operation and Development, *OECD Employment Outlook 2025: Setting the Scene: Demographic Change, Economic Growth and Intergenerational Inequalities* (Paris: OECD Publishing, July 2025), https://www.oecd.org/en/publications/oecd-employment-outlook-2025_194a947b-en/full-report/setting-the-scene-demographic-change-economic-growth-and-intergenerational-inequalities_9d481169.html

10. Shiho Fukada, "For Many of Japan's Elderly Women, Prison Is a Haven," Bloomberg Businessweek, March 16, 2018, https://www.bloomberg.com/news/features/2018-03-16/japan-s-prisons-are-a-haven-for-elderly-women

11. How Japanese prisons are becoming retirement homes for elderly women - Retirement Postponed. https://retirementpostponed.com/life/japanese-prisons/

12. "Crime Hits Record Low in Japan in 2019, but Elderly Offenders on the Rise," *Nippon.com*, June 18, 2020, https://www.nippon.com/en/japan-data/h00749/

13. Fukada, "For Many of Japan's Elderly Women."

14. "Cyrus McCormick," *Encyclopædia Britannica*, accessed December 2024, https://www.britannica.com/biography/Cyrus-McCormick

15. William T. Hutchinson, *Cyrus Hall McCormick: Seed-Time, 1809–1856* (New York: Century Company, 1930), 232–245.

16. "Cyrus McCormick," *Encyclopædia Britannica*.

17. Jannetto, P. J., Laleli-Sahin, E., & Wong, S. H. (2004). Pharmacogenomic genotyping methodologies. Clinical Chemistry and Laboratory Medicine. https://doi.org/10.1515/cclm.2004.246

18. World Economic Forum, *The Future of Jobs Report 2025* (Geneva: World Economic Forum, January 2025), https://www.weforum.org/press/2025/01/future-of-jobs-report-2025-78-million-new-job-opportunities-by-2030-but-urgent-upskilling-needed-to-prepare-workforces/

Chapter 2

1. Dublin, Thomas. *Women at Work: The Transformation of Work and Community in Lowell, Massachusetts, 1826–1860* (New York: Columbia University Press, 1979), 58–59.
2. Thompson, E.P. "Time, Work-Discipline, and Industrial Capitalism." *Past & Present* 38 (1967): 56–97.
3. U.S. National Park Service. "Lucy Larcom."
4. Wikipedia. "Lowell mill girls."
5. Larcom, Lucy. *A New England Girlhood* (Boston: Houghton Mifflin, 1889), 182.
6. Thompson, E.P. "Time, work-discipline, and industrial capitalism." *Past & Present* 38 (1967): 56–97.
7. AFL-CIO. "Lowell Mill Women Create the First Union of Working Women."
8. History Matters. "The Lowell Mill Girls Go on Strike, 1836."
9. Taylor, Frederick Winslow. *The Principles of Scientific Management* (New York: Harper & Brothers, 1911), 43–44.
10. Braverman, Harry. *Labor and Monopoly Capital: The Degradation of Work in the Twentieth Century* (New York: Monthly Review Press, 1974), 112–120.
11. Alliance for Lifetime Income. "Peak 65: How to Navigate the Summit Years." (2024).
12. Bureau of Labor Statistics. "Women in the Labor Force: A Databook." Report 1092 (2021).
13. Bureau of Labor Statistics. "Employee Tenure Summary." News Release USDL-22-1815 (September 20, 2022).
14. Gould, Elise. "State of Working America Wages 2019." Economic Policy Institute (2020).
15. Federal Reserve Bank of St. Louis. "Median Sales Price of Houses Sold." FRED Economic Data (2024).
16. Federal Reserve. "Report on the Economic Well-Being of U.S. Households." (2023).

Chapter 3

1. US Healthcare System, "Q1 2022 Earnings Call Transcript," May 2022.
2. US Healthcare System, "Form 10-Q Quarterly Report," May 6, 2022.

3. NSI Nursing Solutions, "2023 NSI National Health Care Retention & RN Staffing Report," March 2023, https://www.nsinursingsolutions.com/

4. American Organization for Nursing Leadership, "Nursing Leadership Workforce Compendium," 2022, https://www.aonl.org/

5. Kaufman Hall, "The Financial Impact of Contract Labor," February 2023, https://www.kaufmanhall.com/

6. American Association of Colleges of Nursing, "Student Enrollment Surged in U.S. Schools of Nursing in 2021," April 2022, https://www.aacnnursing.org/

7. NSI Nursing Solutions, "2023 NSI National Health Care Retention & RN Staffing Report," March 2023, https://www.nsinursingsolutions.com/

Chapter 4

1. "The U.S. productivity slowdown: an economy-wide and industry-level analysis," U.S. Bureau of Labor Statistics, accessed January 2025, https://www.bls.gov/opub/mlr/2021/article/the-us-productivity-slowdown-the-economy-wide-and-industry-level-analysis.htm

2. Ibid.

3. "How did the monks whose job was to copy books react to Gutenberg's printing press?" History Stack Exchange, accessed January 2025, https://history.stackexchange.com/questions/5552/how-did-the-monks-whose-job-was-to-copy-books-react-to-gutenbergs-printing-pres

4. "The Gutenberg Revolution," Quocirca, accessed January 2025, https://quocirca.com/content/the-gutenberg-revolution-how-the-printing-press-shaped-humanity-and-what-it-means-for-ai/

5. "Global spread of the printing press," Wikipedia, accessed January 2025, https://en.wikipedia.org/wiki/Global_spread_of_the_printing_press

6. "The Gutenberg Press," Oregon State University Libraries, accessed January 2025, https://scarc.library.oregonstate.edu/omeka/exhibits/show/mcdonald/incunabula/gutenberg/

7. "How Long It Took for a Medieval Monk to Copy a Book," The History Ace, accessed January 2025, https://thehistoryace.com/how-long-it-took-for-a-medieval-monk-to-copy-a-book/

8. Ibid.

9. "History of rail transportation in the United States," Wikipedia, accessed January 2025, https://en.wikipedia.org/wiki/History_of_rail_transportation_in_the_United_States

10. "The Power of Exponential Thinking," Peter Diamandis Blog, accessed January 2025, https://www.diamandis.com/blog/scaling-abundance-series-13

11. Levy and Tasoff, "Exponential-growth bias and overconfidence," *Journal of Economic Psychology* 58 (2016), https://www.researchgate.net/publication/309876862_Exponential-Growth_Bias_and_Overconfidence

12. "The neuroscience basis of mathematical cognitive impairment," Frontiers in Psychology, 2023, https://www.frontiersin.org/journals/psychology/articles/10.3389/fpsyg.2023.1282957/full

13. "Barriers to Change: Status Quo Bias," NOBL, accessed January 2025, https://nobl.io/changemaker/change-barriers-status-quo-bias/

14. Automation Anywhere. "Automation Anywhere's Generative AI-Powered Automation Saves a Brazilian Energy Company $120 Million in Just Three Weeks." Press release. Automation Anywhere. March 7, 2024.

15. Ibid. The press release notes: "The company is planning to use the savings to help the company transition to sustainable forms of energy over the coming years and has a strategy to develop renewable energy, including wind and solar."

Chapter 5

1. "AI Best Bets: Accelerate Automation with AI," Automation Anywhere Webinar, accessed January 2025.

2. "Deep Blue | IBM," accessed January 2025, https://www.ibm.com/history/deep-blue

3. "Deep Blue versus Garry Kasparov," Wikipedia, accessed January 2025, https://en.wikipedia.org/wiki/Deep_Blue_versus_Garry_Kasparov

4. "Tips for parents | Delancey UK Schools' Chess Challenge." https://www.delanceyukschoolschesschallenge.com/category/tips-for-parents/

5. "Twenty years on from Deep Blue vs Kasparov: how a chess match started the big data revolution," The Conversation, accessed January 2025, https://theconversation.com/twenty-years-on-from-deep-blue-vs-kasparov-how-a-chess-match-started-the-big-data-revolution-76882

6. "AlphaGo—Google DeepMind," accessed January 2025, https://deepmind.google/research/breakthroughs/alphago/

7. "Lee Sedol versus AlphaGo," Christopher Roosen, accessed January 2025, https://www.christopherroosen.com/blog/2019/12/1/lee-sedol-

versus-alphago-human-meaning-in-games-as-we-enter-the-age-of-artificial-intelligence

8. "AlphaGo | Reflections and Quotes," vialogue, accessed January 2025, https://vialogue.wordpress.com/2018/02/16/alphago-reflections-and-quotes/

9. "Lee Sedol versus AlphaGo," Christopher Roosen, accessed January 2025.

10. "DALL-E," Wikipedia, accessed January 2025, https://en.wikipedia.org/wiki/DALL-E

11. "Technical Performance," Stanford HAI 2025 AI Index, accessed January 2025, https://hai.stanford.edu/ai-index/2025-ai-index-report/technical-performance

12. "Technical Performance," Stanford HAI 2025 AI Index.

13. Ibid.

14. "Resistance to Medical AI," Harvard Business School Working Knowledge, November 14, 2023, https://hbswk.hbs.edu/item/resistance-to-medical-ai

15. "Resistance to Medical AI," Harvard Business School Working Knowledge.

16. UniverseLair, "We're Not Ready For Self Driving Cars 🚗 w/ Neil deGrasse Tyson," YouTube video, 0:48, July 30, 2025, https://youtube.com/shorts/6cV92awSR3I?feature=shared

17. "Mayo Clinic's Healthy Model for AI Success," MIT Sloan Management Review, accessed January 2025, https://sloanreview.mit.edu/article/mayo-clinics-healthy-model-for-ai-success/

18. "Mayo Clinic trial signals potential for AI-guided heart disease detection," Healthcare IT News, accessed January 2025, https://www.healthcareitnews.com/news/mayo-clinic-trial-signals-potential-ai-guided-heart-disease-detection

19. "Mayo Clinic's John Halamka: 'We have to use AI'," Chief Healthcare Executive, accessed January 2025, https://www.chiefhealthcareexecutive.com/view/mayo-clinic-s-john-halamka-we-have-to-use-ai-

20. "Goldman Sachs rolls out an AI assistant for its employees," CNBC, January 21, 2025, https://www.cnbc.com/2025/01/21/goldman-sachs-launches-ai-assistant.html

21. "Goldman Sachs CEO says that AI can draft 95% of an IPO prospectus in minutes," Fortune, January 17, 2025, https://fortune.com/2025/01/17/goldman-sachs-ceo-david-solomon-ai-tasks-ipo-prospectus-s1-filing-sec/

22. "How Toyota is revolutionizing manufacturing with AI," Google Cloud Blog, accessed January 2025, https://cloud.google.com/blog/

23. "Toyota: Fostering Widespread AI Adoption," Dataiku, accessed January 2025, https://www.dataiku.com/stories/detail/toyota/

24. "When humans and AI work best together," MIT Sloan, accessed January 2025, https://mitsloan.mit.edu/

25. "A US Newspaper ignites Agentic AI to pioneer transformative media monetization strategies with speed and scale," Automation Anywhere Case Study, July 2025.

26. "A Leading US Newspaper ignites Agentic AI to pioneer transformative media monetization strategies with speed and scale," Automation Anywhere Case Study, July 2025.

27. "Redefining Business Performance with a Leading US Newspaper at Imagine 2025," Automation Anywhere, accessed January 2025.

28. "AI Best Bets: Accelerate Automation with AI," Automation Anywhere Webinar, accessed January 2025.

29. "A Leading US Newspaper ignites Agentic AI to pioneer transformative media monetization strategies with speed and scale," Automation Anywhere Case Study, July 2025.

30. Ibid.

Chapter 6

1. Global Professional Services Company Case Study, "Automation Anywhere," 2025.

2. Ibid.

3. "The science behind successful organizational transformations," McKinsey & Company. https://www.mckinsey.com/capabilities/people-and-organizational-performance/our-insights/successful-transformations

4. "Changing change management," McKinsey & Company. https://www.mckinsey.com/featured-insights/leadership/changing-change-management

5. "How JPMorgan Uses AI to Save 360,000 Legal Hours a Year," Medium, May 16, 2025. https://medium.com/@arahmedraza/how-jpmorgan-uses-ai-to-save-360-000-legal-hours-a-year-6e94d58a557b

6. "Transforming Work: Gartner's AI Predictions Through 2029," SHRM. https://www.shrm.org/topics-tools/flagships/ai-hi/gartner-ai-predictions-through-2029

7. "Amazon's Two Pizza Teams," AWS Executive Insights. https://aws.amazon.com/executive-insights/content/amazon-two-pizza-team/

8. "Satya Nadella returned Microsoft to the top by showing humility as CEO," Fortune. https://fortune.com/2024/09/30/microsoft-ceo-satya-nadella-leadership-success-humility-culture-change/

9. "How Satya Nadella navigated Microsoft to $3 trillion market value," Computerworld. https://www.computerworld.com/article/1611671/how-satya-nadella-navigated-microsoft-to-3-trillion-market-value.html

10. "Reinventing Best Buy—Case," Harvard Business School. https://www.hbs.edu/faculty/Pages/item.aspx?num=50946

11. "How AT&T Employees Turned Process Gripes into $230 Million Saved," MIT Sloan Management Review, December 12, 2024. https://sloanreview.mit.edu/article/how-att-employees-turned-process-gripes-into-230-million-saved/

12. "Tesla is now worth more than GM, Ford, Toyota, and other car companies—combined," Yahoo Tech, November 13, 2024. https://tech.yahoo.com/transportation/articles/tesla-worth-more-gm-ford-195100423.html

Chapter 7

1. RingCentral, "Workers Waste Up to 1 Day Per Work Week on Inefficient Collaboration," 2023, https://www.ringcentral.com/us/en/blog/workers-toggle-between-apps-9-times-daily/

2. Mass Moments, "'Mill Girl' Writer Lucy Larcom Dies," https://www.massmoments.org/moment-details/mill-girl-writer-lucy-larcom% of the license fee -dies.html

3. Pemeco Consulting, "Two Big Reasons for ERP Implementation Failure," https://pemeco.com/two-big-reasons-erp-implementation-failure/; Genius ERP, "ERP Price Guide: How Much Does a Manufacturing ERP System Cost?" https://www.geniuserp.com/resources/blog/erp-system-cost/

4. Automation Anywhere, "Global Food and Agriculture Leader Case Study: Less Than a Minute, More Than $10M Saved," 2025,

5. Leila Shahrzadi et al., "Causes, Consequences, and Strategies to Deal With Information Overload: A Scoping Review," *International Journal of Information Management Data Insights* 4, no. 2 (June 21, 2024): 100261, https://doi.org/10.1016/j.jjimei.2024.100261.

6. "Human Centered Design (HCD) | NIST," NIST, May 3, 2021, https://www.nist.gov/itl/iad/visualization-and-usability-group/human-factors-human-centered-design

7. IxDF, "5 Stages in the Design Thinking Process," https://www.interaction-design.org/literature/article/5-stages-in-the-design-thinking-process

8. Automation Anywhere, "Global Food and Agriculture Leader Case Study: What's Next," 2025.

Chapter 8

1. "Quarterback Leadership Research: The Quarterback as Outcome-Focused Manager," research report for *The 5-Year Century*, 2025.

2. "Quarterback Leadership Research," NFL roster volatility analysis showing 56.4% annual player turnover and 35.1% two-year retention rates.

3. Boston Consulting Group, "Move Fast, Scale Smart: AI-First Companies Win the Future," BCG *Executive Perspectives* (June 2025), 9, https://image-src.bcg.com/Images/bcg-executive-perspectives-ai-first-companies-win-the-future-issue1-10june2025_tcm9-398876.pdf

4. BCG, "Move Fast, Scale Smart," 3–5.

5. "Self-Organizing Workforces," section noting that queen bees exercise no executive function, produce only eggs and pheromones signaling presence, and make zero operational decisions about colony operations.

6. "Self-Organizing Workforces," section on worker bee age polytheism describing the standard progression from internal work (cell cleaning, nursing, comb building, food processing) to external foraging over five to seven week lifespans.

7. "Self-Organizing Workforces," section on worker bee role flexibility, citing single-cohort experiments showing some individuals beginning foraging at four to seven days old, three weeks earlier than normal, while others delayed transitions.

8. "Self-Organizing Workforces," section on communication enabling coordination without centralized control, describing how approximately 500 scout bees search independently for potential nest sites during swarming.

9. "Self-Organizing Workforces," section on Thomas Seeley's research on nest site selection, noting that once thirty to forty scouts accumulate at a single site (a quorum threshold), commitment accelerates to conclusion without any queen or elite individual directing the process.

10. "Value Proposition for Project Beehive at Automation Anywhere," internal document, 2025, describing the initiative as redesigning how leadership works by transitioning from traditional people managers to a

dynamic, project-led model that empowers individuals to lead based on expertise, centralizes HR services and employment decisions, uses intelligent agents for training and coaching, and ensures expert support is available when needed.

11. Amy Edmondson's psychological safety research as documented in "Growth Mindset Organizational Flexibility Research."

12. "Growth Mindset Organizational Flexibility Research," noting that higher-performing teams report more errors because they discuss them.

13. BCG, "Move Fast, Scale Smart," 5, documenting that AI-first companies achieve 25–35X traditional baseline in revenue per employee.

Chapter 9

1. Huntsman Savile Row, "Bespoke Tailoring," https://www.huntsmansa vilerow.com/pages/bespoke-tailoring

2. Jasper Littman, "A History of Savile Row," December 7, 2020, https:// jasperlittman.com/a-history-of-savile-row/; Alexandra Wood, "A Guide to Savile Row Tailoring," January 17, 2025, https://alexandrawoodbe spoke.co.uk/blogs/bespoke-made-to-measure-tailoring/a-guide-to-savile-row-tailoring-everything-you-need-to-know/

3. Esquire UK, "The Ultimate Insider's Guide to All the Tailors on Savile Row," August 15, 2023, https://www.esquire.com/uk/style/a31209353/savile-row-tailors/

4. Benjamin's Custom NYC, "3D Body Scanning," https://www.benjamins custom.com/custom-3d-body-scanning.html

5. 3DLOOK, "Mobile Tailor," February 28, 2025, https://3dlook.ai/mobile-tailor/

6. Tailorized, "AI-Powered 3D Body Scanning Technology," https://tailorized.ai/

7. Esquire UK, "The Ultimate Insider's Guide to All the Tailors on Savile Row," August 15, 2023, https://www.esquire.com/uk/style/a31209353/savile-row-tailors/

8. Automation Anywhere, "Human Capital and Benefits Services Provider Case Study," 2025,

9. Ibid.

10. The Texas Tribune, "Printing a place to live: In Central Texas, homes are being built with emerging 3D technology," October 6, 2023, https://www.texastribune.org/2023/10/06/texas-houses-3D-printers-climate/

11. Ibid.

12. Xometry, Inc., "Xometry Reports Fourth Quarter and Full Year 2024 Results," February 26, 2025, https://investors.xometry.com/news-releases/news-release-details/xometry-reports-fourth-quarter-and-full-year-2024-results

13. Progressive, "Progressive Introduces Usage-Based Insurance and Fleet Management Program for Business Owners," December 8, 2020, https://www.prnewswire.com/news-releases/progressive-introduces-usage-based-insurance-and-fleet-management-program-for-business-owners-301188373.html

14. Ibid.

15. Wikipedia, "NikeID," https://en.wikipedia.org/wiki/NikeID

16. Wikipedia, "Mass Customization," https://en.wikipedia.org/wiki/Mass_customization

17. Pine, *Mass Customization*, Harvard Business School Press, 1993

18. Rebuy, "How Netflix Uses Personalization," https://www.rebuyengine.com/blog/netflix

19. ShipBob, "Case Studies," https://www.shipbob.com/case-studies/

20. SkyQuest, "AI-Based Personalization Market," https://www.skyquestt.com/report/artificial-intelligence-based-personalization-market

21. Automation Anywhere, "Human Capital and Benefits Services Provider Case Study," 2025

22. Ibid.

23. The Climate Corporation, "Improved FieldView Experience in 2024 Includes New Connectivity Option with Precision Planting," January 16, 2024, https://climate.com/en-us/resources/press-releases/improved-fieldview-experience-in-2024-includes-new-connectivity-option-with-precision-planting.html

24. Geisinger, "Geisinger's MyCode Community Health Initiative hits milestone, enrolls 300,000 participants," April 6, 2022, https://www.geisinger.org/about-geisinger/news-and-media/news-releases/2022/04/06/13/43/mycode-community-health-initiative-hits-milestone

25. Coca-Cola Solutions, "Personalize Guest Experiences with Coca-Cola Freestyle," https://www.cokesolutions.com/coca-cola-freestyle/articles/personalize-guest-experiences-with-coca-cola-freestyle.html

26. Human Capital and Benefits Services Provider Customer at Imagine 2025, Interview Transcript

27. Ibid.

28. Automation Anywhere, "Industry-First Generative AI," https://www
.automationanywhere.com/company/press-room/automation-
anywheres-industry-first-generative-ai-powered-process-automation

Chapter 10

1. John Woolman, *The Journal of John Woolman* (1774; modern edition).
2. Thomas D. Hamm, *The Quakers in America* (Columbia University Press, 2003).
3. "Accelerating a UK Healthcare System's Workforce Transformation with AI-Powered Automation," Automation Anywhere, August 6, 2024
4. "Enron files for bankruptcy," HISTORY, December 2, 2001, https://www .history.com/this-day-in-history/enron-files-for-bankruptcy; "The Business Case for a High-Trust Culture," Great Place to Work Research Report, 2024, https://www.greatplacetowork.com/resources/reports/the-business-case-for-high-trust-culture
5. "Enron Stock Price Chart and Data," Famous Trials, accessed January 2025, https://famous-trials.com/enron/1791-stockchart
6. 2026 Edelman Trust Barometer, https://www.edelman.com/trust/2026/ trust-barometer
7. Paul J. Zak, "The Neuroscience of Trust," Harvard Business Review, January-February 2017, https://hbr.org/2017/01/the-neuroscience-of-trust
8. Ibid.
9. "Building Trust in Industry: Lessons from Patagonia," Your Comms Group, 2024, https://yourcommsgroup.com/case-study/building-trust-patagonia-strategies/
10. "How Patagonia Enhances Customer Experience," Renascence, 2024, https://www.renascence.io/journal/how-patagonia-enhances-customer-experience-cx-with-a-commitment-to-sustainability
11. "Costco ACTUAL Pay and Salary (2025)," Bandana Resources, 2025, https://resources.bandana.com/resources/costco-actual-pay-and-salary-2024
12. "Costco Human Resources: What You Need to Know," The Human Capital Hub, 2024, https://www.thehumancapitalhub.com/articles/costco-human-resources-what-you-need-to-know
13. "Employee Trust Fuels Financial Success at the 100 Best Companies to Work For in 2025," Morningstar, 2025, https://www.morningstar.com/news/globe-newswire/9414054/employee-trust-fuels-financial-success-at-the-100-best-companies-to-work-for-in-2025

14. "Accelerating a UK Healthcare System's Workforce Transformation with AI-Powered Automation," Automation Anywhere, August 6, 2024
15. Ibid.

Chapter 11

1. Raj Joshi and Robert Burgelman, "Automation Anywhere in 2023: 100 Million Digital Workers and Counting," Stanford Graduate School of Business Case Study SM-373, November 6, 2023, p. 2.
2. Ibid.
3. Ibid.
4. Ibid.

Index